FINE CHOCOLATES, GREAT EXPERIENCE /

© Uitgeverij Lannoo nv, Tielt – 2004

fourth printrun

ISBN 978-90-209-5914-7
D 2008/45/ 132 - NUR 441

TEXT: Jean-Pierre Wybauw
PHOTOGRAPHY: Tony Le Duc
DESIGN: Maarten Pollet
EDITING: Txt-Pro, Anne-Marie Recour
TRANSLATION: Lyrco

Printed and bound by Printer Trento Srl, Trento, Italy - 2008

Contents

PREFACE   *7*

JEAN-PIERRE WYBAUW, A CHOCOLATE WIZARD   *8*

SWEET IMPRESSIONS OF A FEW MASTER CHOCOLATIERS   *10*

A WORD OF THANKS   *13*

CHARACTERISTICS OF THE MOST FREQUENTLY USED INGREDIENTS   *15*

CHOCOLATE PROCESSING   *32*

RHEOLOGY   *44*

SHELF LIFE AND FACTORS THAT EXTEND SHELF LIFE   *48*

SUGAR PROCESSING   *57*

STARTING OUT   *65*

PRALINE RECIPES BASED ON NUTS   *83*

FAT-BASED RECIPES   *100*

GANACHES   *113*

CARAMELS   *165*

NOUGAT   *175*

FRUIT-IN-LIQUEUR CHOCOLATES   *178*

MARZIPAN AND PERSIPAN   *185*

TRUFFLES AND CHOCOLATE TRUFFLE BALLS   *191*

FRUIT DOUGH   *212*

MISCELLANEOUS   *216*

Preface

Quite a few specialist books have been published in which the focus has mainly been on recipes and beautiful images. This is often at the expense of the book's usefulness in a professional environment. Hence the need to write a specialist book that is intended as a manual focussed mainly on technique. The premise is that beginners as well as experienced professionals will be able to use this book as a guideline.

Traditional topics such as the history of chocolate, the origin of cocoa and the production of chocolate are not addressed in this book, as there are many publications already available on these subjects. This book is practical and is mainly intended for regular consultation by users whilst they are at work.

Processing chocolate looks quite simple at first sight; however, there are several factors that must be respected to achieve successful products with a respectable shelf life. This is why the various processes are explained and illustrated in a rational manner. With an improved knowledge of ingredients it is easier to develop new recipes.

In addition to providing clear technical information, the book also offers help in finding solutions to problems and in extending the shelf life of the products, a worrying subject for many a chocolatier. In this work I have also tried to create a variety of recipes and I have chosen to provide several working methods. There are ganache recipes for which the cooked cream is poured on the finely chopped chocolate, while in other recipes the cooked cream is first cooled and only then poured on the pre-crystallised chocolate.

Quite deliberately I have sometimes opted for sorbitol, or salt, or sodium bicarbonate or other ingredients. Sometimes an ingredient can be replaced or just left out, and sometimes its use is essential. The reason for this varied approach is to enable readers to improve their knowledge on how to apply these ingredients and recognise their usefulness. The choice of flavours used is a very personal one. They can be replaced by other flavours.

The Aw value is indicated for most recipes. This is unique in specialist literature on chocolate products. The Aw value gives you an idea of shelf life, providing correct treatment and storage are taken into consideration (Refer to chapters on water activity and shelf life).

JEAN-PIERRE WYBAUW

Jean-Pierre Wybauw, a chocolate wizard

Jean-PierreWybauw is one of those personalities we would like to meet more often in the chocolate industry. Not only is he a mine of information on all things chocolate, he is also a very kind hearted man, always available and willing to share his knowledge. He is admired by an entire generation of apprentice chocolatiers.

He is a true enthusiast, whose in-depth knowledge of the trade is matched by a passion to communicate this know-how to as many people as possible. His current work promises to be a benchmark for the future.

To those who meet him, Jean-Pierre manages to convey his great love of chocolate as an object of sweetness, his fondness for food and his ebullient and dynamic nature – the very essence of his profession as a chocolatier.

At the time of our last meeting I was a mere adolescent and his impressive chocolate sculpture displays at "Euroba" will be forever engraved upon my memory and were the inspiration of my vocation as a chocolatier. His chocolate sculptures are delicate and fleeting masterpieces, expressions of art based on sweetness and contrasts, admired by amateurs and professionals alike.

During our meetings Jean-Pierre introduced me to the brotherhood of which he was a product, the Richmont Club of Belgium whose members included the elite of Belgian patissiers. These individuals, whom I longed to emulate, not only provided a range of extraordinary know-how but also presented a noble and passionate vision of the trade. This was based on continually evolving creativity and respect for the artisan's craft – something I still defend with the same gusto to this day.

Jean-Pierre Wybauw is much more than a mere representative of this elite. He is, most definitely, a figurehead since his talent and love of the profession continue to be an example for new generations of chocolatiers, keen to learn and discover the alchemic secrets of this wonderful trade. Because of his modesty, listening skills and accessibility for young up and coming talent, Jean-Pierre Wybauw could be considered an open book on the profession of chocolatier.

I feel it an honour to be able to express my gratitude and admiration today to a man whose dynamic nature has introduced me to the magic of chocolate, its technical secrets and expressive power. I hope that readers of this book will gain as much pleasure from browsing through its pages as I had discovering the many facets of Jean-Pierre Wybauw's personality.

PIERRE MARCOLINI, Master Chocolatier of Belgium

Sweet impressions of a few master chocolatiers

JACQUY PFEIFFER is co-owner of the *French Pastry School* in Chicago with Sebastien Canonne. Jacquy won his first title at the age of 17, and has since gathered quite a collection of titles and medals. He has worked in top hotels, as executive pastry chef for the Saudi Royal family as well as for his royal highness the Sultan of Brunei.

This year SEBASTIEN CANONNE has earned the prestigious title of "Meilleur ouvrier de France". He has worked in top hotels and at the Palais de l'Elysée in Paris for President François Mitterand. He has earned many prizes and medals during his career.

Finally, a book about chocolate that is an indispensable tool for all chocolatiers, both beginners and professionals. While working with chocolate seems fun and easy, an in-depth knowledge of the chemistry of chocolate is essential to achieve a consistent, smooth and delectable product. The composition of raw products is explained so that you will be able to formulate your own chocolate candy recipes. This chocolate bible provides the answers to all your possible troubleshooting questions.

JACQUY PFEIFFER

JACQUES TORRES is the owner of Jacques Torres Chocolate in New York, and also holds the prestigious title of "Meilleur ouvrier de France". Jacques has had his own TV show in the United States for several years. He also wrote two professional books: *Dessert Circus At Home* and *Dessert Circus Extraordinary Desserts You Can Make At Home* and is currenty working on his third book.

Finally, a book that is both attractive and technical....an indispensable tool to help professionals understand and master the complexity of chocolate. Jean-Pierre shares his passion and the knowledge of a long career. I highly recommend it!

Jacques Torres

THOMAS GUMPEL is Associate Dean of Baking and Pastry Arts *The Culinary Institute of America*.

At last a book that professional chocolatiers can call their own. Jean-Pierre Wybauw, otherwise known as Mr. Chocolate, has come through with the ultimate text on chocolate. I find myself very fortunate being able to scan through the pages of Mr.

Wybauw's life long experience. With each page comes a wealth of information from the basics of chocolate to the in depth interactions of ingredients within a ganache. The photos are stunning and the information is laid out in a clear, concise manner. This is one of the few books that will remain at my bedside and upon my work bench.

T S Gumpel

ALBERT ADRIA is co-owner of the world's top restaurant El Bulli and author of 'Los Postres de El Bulli', which was voted best pastry book of the year in 1998. Albert gives demonstrations throughout the world.

At the end of November 2003 Jean-Pierre mentioned to me that he was finally going to write his own book, an idea that had occurred to him many years before. I knew straight away that this was not going to be just another book, one of the many already dedicated to chocolate. Those of us who know him, and his struggles between various exhibitions, are also familiar with his knowledge, composure and professionalism, which are equalled by his passion for his vocation.
Specialisation, perspective, technique, functionality and rationality in particular (all qualities that define him as a person) must have been on his mind even before he had written his first word.
As you will see it is an inexhaustible source of ideas and will be appreciated by those who, like me, are looking for something more than just recipes in a book.

EWALD NOTTER is the owner of the *Notter School of Pastry Arts* in Orlando, Florida. Ewald is an expert in sugar processing and wins just about every contest in which he participates. As a result he holds a record number of gold medals. Ewald organises courses and demonstrations worldwide and has written two books, '*Sugar Pulling and Sugar Blowing*' and '*Das ist Zucker*' (That is Sugar).

Jean-Pierre Wybauw is an extremely talented chocolatier, with a passion for his profession. His thought provoking and inspiring work ethic is evident throughout his book, a significant and vast addition to the range. Jean-Pierre shares his mouthwatering recipes and know-how with those seeking a more in-depth and extended knowledge of chocolate.

MARC DEBAILLEUL is a member of the "Academie Culinaire de France", was awarded the prestigious title of "Meilleur Ouvrier de France" (Best Master Craftsman in France). Marc is the winner of several trade contests and owner of the top of the range patisserie chain, *Debailleul Products*, with outlets in Brussels, Osaka and Tokyo.

This book is an excellent tool and guide for all enthusiasts who want to work with the splendid substance that is chocolate. It is also an accomplished masterpiece as a record of Jean-Pierre's entire career – the career of a discrete, humble and passionate professional. I hope this book will help its many readers to find solutions to the countless questions they are likely to encounter along their professional paths. I can only recommend that those who love to work with chocolate consult it regularly and would like to send my heartfelt congratulations to its author!

MARC DEBAILLEUL

RUDOLPH VAN VEEN, *Netherlands Patisserie Team*, TV-chef "Life & Cooking"

Chocolate has been an inspiration for centuries as one of the most fascinating luxury foods. Some people turn their passion for chocolate into a profession. Jean-Pierre Wybauw is a typical example of this. He seems to have liquid chocolate rather than blood running through his veins. He EXUDES chocolate! During the National and World Party Team Championships in the United States I got to know Jean-Pierre as an unassuming, modest professional. He prefers to give rather than receive, as demonstrated by this wonderful book.

The best way to thank Jean-Pierre for his knowledge and energy is to use and consult the book as often as possible. If your copy becomes well thumbed and smudged with chocolate after a while, it will be a silent testimonial to the book's merit.

Rudolph

A word of thanks

I would like to thank the following companies for believing in my project from the very beginning. They have provided enormous moral support and their faith enabled me to produce this first book.

CALLEBAUT Aalstersestraat 122 B-9280 Lebbeke-Wieze, Belgium
www.ecallebaut.be
For sponsoring and use of the workshop at the Callebaut Academy.

MOL D'ART Industriepark 16. B-3290 Webbekom-Diest, Belgium
www.moldart.be

BROTHERS DEDY GMBH Frankenstrasse 152, D-4300 Essen 1, Germany
www.dedy.de

ROBOT COUPE 26,rue des Hayettes. B-6540 Mont-Sainte-Genevieve, Belgium
dufour.gérard@robot-coupe.be

CLS RÉMY COINTREAU 152, Avenue des Champs Elysées, F-75008 Paris, France
pierre.pesret@rémy-cointreau.com

AMORETTI NOUSHIG,INC. 10021-1/2 Canoga Avenue Chatsworth, CA 91311 - USA
www.amoretti.com

I also owe a debt of gratitude to Dirk De Schepper and Luc Rooms, the former and current head managers of the analytical labs at Callebaut, for the information they provided me with.

A special thank you to Tony Le Duc for his superb photography and agreeable cooperation.

Thank you!

JEAN-PIERRE WYBAUW

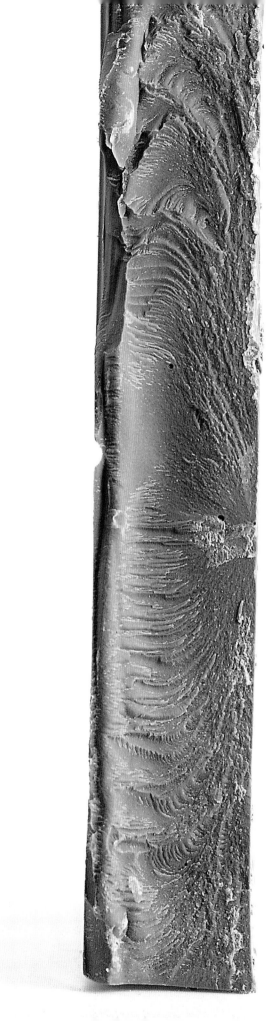

01

Characteristics
of the most frequently used ingredients

Cacao ingredients *16* / Milk products *19* / Nuts *20* / Fats *20* / Sugars *22* /
Other sweeteners *23* / Additives *26* / Thickeners and whipping agents *26* /
Whipping agents *28* / Spice mixtures *29* / Flavours *29* /

Each ingredient has its own specific characteristics. Some ingredients protect the recipe against drying or extend its shelf life.

When various ingredients are combined in a recipe, some blend well but others, such as fats and water, do not.

Recipe creators should understand the characteristics of their ingredients and ensure that the recipes are based on a "good marriage".

Cocoa ingredients

CHOCOLATE / **Chocolate is a dispersion of fine particles of solids (cocoa, sugar and milk powder) in cocoa butter.** The term "chocolate" must meet legal requirements, but almost all countries have their own standards for chocolate. Furthermore, international standards are laid down by the Food and Agricultural Organisation of the United Nations (FAO) and the World Health Organisation (WHO) in the Codex Alimentarius. That is why it is not relevant to give figures. Roughly speaking all dark chocolates contain at least 30-35% cocoa components, and at least 18% cocoa butter. A quality reference contains at least 26% cocoa butter. Chocolate coating at least 31%. Milk chocolate contains 20-25% cocoa components.

Milk chocolate also contains milk fat, i.e. the total of cocoa butter and milk fat. This is why household milk chocolate should contain a total of at least 25% fat. Milk chocolate coating a total of at least 31% fat.

White chocolate contains at least 20% cocoa butter and 12-14% milk components.

Because of the high cocoa/butter ratio the name "couverture" refers to quality aspects that result in:
- Better melting in the mouth;
- More pleasant and richer experience (not as dry);
- Better snap;
- Higher degree of liquidity upon processing;
- Higher cost price.

When putting together recipes in which chocolate is processed, some factors need to be taken into account.

FOR DARK CHOCOLATE
- Dry cocoa components give the (bitter) chocolate taste and colour;
- The sugar in the chocolate makes the recipe sweeter;
- The cocoa butter determines the firmness of the centre.

FOR MILK CHOCOLATE
- Dry cocoa components give the chocolate flavour;
- The sugar makes the recipe sweeter than when using dark chocolate, since the strong and bitter cocoa taste is significantly toned down by the high milk content;
- Milk fats influence the structure: they create a smooth effect, since milk fat is much smoother than cocoa butter;
- The behaviour of cocoa butter is very much influenced by the blending of various fats.

FOR WHITE CHOCOLATE
- Sugar determines the sweetness of the recipe;
- Milk powders create a full, creamy flavour;
- The combination of cocoa butter and milk fat give a smooth effect;
- The behaviour of cocoa butter is very much influenced by the blending of various fats.

Consequently, the choice of chocolate is not the only important factor, the portion of cocoa butter the chocolate contains is also significant.

FOR EXAMPLE
- Hazelnuts contain approximately 64% oil
- Standard dark chocolate contains approximately 35% cocoa butter
- Standard milk chocolate contains approximately 30% cocoa butter
- Standard white chocolate contains approximately 28% cocoa butter
- Praliné paste contains 50% sugar and 50% hazelnuts

1,000 g praliné mixed with 500 g dark chocolate containing approximately 35% cocoa butter has an nice soft yet sliceable texture. 320 g nut oil was mixed with 175 g cocoa butter.

With the use of 30% milk chocolate the butter fat contained in this chocolate is taken into account. In order to obtain the same texture as with dark chocolate 60%

milk chocolate must now be added to 1,000 g praliné. When using white chocolate 70% chocolate is added to 1,000 g praliné.

NIBS / Nibs are cleaned cocoa beans, free from bacteria, roasted and chopped into fragments. They have a strong taste and add flavour and aroma to centres. They are used in centres to give a crunchy effect and give sweet centres a bittersweet balance. They are also used for finishing.

COCOA MASS OR CACAO LIQUEUR / 100% cleaned cocoa beans, free from bacteria, roasted, broken and then finely ground. Since cocoa beans are very rich in cocoa butter (approx. 55%) a very liquid, dark brown, bitter and somewhat sour paste is obtained after grinding. An ideal product to give a strong cocoa flavour to centres, with little influence on texture.

COCOA BUTTER / Cocoa butter is a product of the cocoa bean, which can contain up to 55% cocoa butter.

Taste, odour, solidifying behaviour and hardness can differ, depending on origin. This is how the taste can vary from no cocoa taste (neutral) to palpable cocoa taste and how Malay cocoa butter is noticeably harder than Brazilian butter. Cocoa butter gives gloss, hardness and shrinkage to the chocolate. The higher the cocoa butter content in the chocolate, the more attractive the appearance of the end product. When producing pralines cocoa butter is used to:

- dilute the chocolate (for extra thin cover or spraying with airbrush);
- harden centres, without making them sweeter (as by adding chocolate);
- mix with fat soluble colouring agents (to colour chocolate);
- protect marzipan against drying out (by covering with thin coat of cocoa butter).

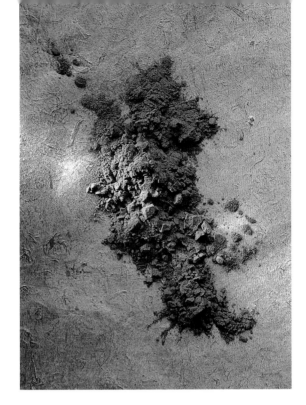

COCOA POWDER / Cocoa powder is the (partially) dry substance that remains after separating cocoa butter from the cocoa mass. Cocoa powder is used for its taste as well as its colour. There is a difference between:

- Low fat cocoa powder (contains approximately 10-12% cocoa butter);
- Whole cocoa powder (contains approximately 20-22% cocoa butter). American terminology differs from British terminology.
- Alkalised cocoa powder (alkalising means making alkaline or neutralising sour taste). Alkalising darkens the cocoa powder and makes it more easily soluble in a watery environment;
- Non-alkalised cocoa powder (makes creams or ganaches curdle more rapidly).

Milk products

CREAM / Cream is an emulsion of fat in water. Cream contains at least 30% fat (ideally about 40%) and about 60% water. Cream has a shelf life of approximately one week. Because of its high water content it provides creams with a light and smooth texture, but also with a limited shelf life. Combined with the right ingredients, the shelf life can be considerably extended. Blending with the wrong ingredients changes the texture after a

short period (drying out, recrystallising, moistening) and results in a limited shelf life.

SWEETENED CONDENSED MILK / Low fat condensed milk consists of 27.5% water, 0.2% fat, 20.8% fat-free milk solids and 45.5% sugar. Whole condensed milk consists of 25.5% water, 9.1% fat, 22.9% fat-free milk solids and 42.5% sugar.

MILK POWDER / Whole condensed milk consists of 25.5% water, 9.1% fat, 22.9% fat-free milk solids and 42.5% sugar. The latter is preferable as it dissolves more easily and is finer. Low fat milk powder contains a maximum of 5% water and at least 95% fat-free milk solids. Whole milk powder contains a maximum of 5% water, at least 25-30% fat and 70% fat-free milk solids.

BUTTER / Butter is an emulsion of fat in water. Butter contains at least 82% fat and a maximum of 16% water. Butter has a shelf life of about two to three months. Because of its high soft fat content butter has a soft to solid, fat texture. Recipes in which cream is replaced with butter, extend the shelf life of the product.

Nuts

Nuts and nut products are used frequently in chocolate processing. They are very rich in oil. Because these oils strongly influence the structure of the centre, it is useful to know the average oil percentage in the most widely used nuts.

Almonds	55%
Brazil nuts	65%
Cashews	44%
Coconuts	57%
Hazelnuts	64%
Macadamia nuts	74%
Peanuts	44%
Pecans	70%
Pistachios	55%
Sweet chestnuts	8%
Walnuts	61%

Oils even stay liquid at very low temperatures, therefore attention must be paid to fat migration in chocolate when using nuts.

Fats

Warning: Inexpert use of fats in chocolate products can lead to huge problems. Vegetable fats are discussed extensively below, but also milk fat of animal origin.

COMPOSITION /   **Fat molecules are made up of glycerol and three fatty acids.** There are a great number of fatty acids:
  ~ With various chain lengths: short - long
  ~ With different saturation points for long fatty acids. Fats are always a mixture of several fat molecules due to the existing fatty acid combination. Owing to this, fat has no clear melting point, but a more or less extensive melting path.

CHARACTERISTICS /   **Fats with many short fatty acids have a relatively low melting path**
  ~ Coconut oil: 10-25°C (50-77°F)
Fats with many long fatty acids that are quite heavily saturated have a relatively high melting path
  ~ Cocoa butter 25-35°C (77-95°F)
Fats with many long fatty acids that are quite heavily unsaturated have a relatively low melting path
  ~ Soybean oil: -30-0°C (-22-32°F)
The simpler the fat composition the shorter the melting path
  ~ Cocoa butter 25-35°C (77-95°F)
The more complex the fat composition the longer the melting path
  ~ Milk fat: 0-40°C (32-104°F)

ADAPTATION CHARACTERISTICS /   **The fat industry has developed methods for adjusting physical characteristics of fats to specific applications**
  ~ Fractionation: Fats are separated by crystallisation in higher and lower melting fractions. This is a purely physical process whereby fat molecules do not undergo any chemical change.
  ~ Hardening: Through chemical changes in the fat molecules' unsaturated fatty acids the melting point can be increased to a greater or lesser degree.

COMPATIBILITY /   **The more chemically similar fats are, the more compatible they are.** Nut oil and almond oil are examples of this. The more divergent their chemical composition, the less compatible they are. Cocoa butter and milk fat are examples of this. Incompatibility causes abnormally low melting paths.

FAT GROUPS /

LAURIC FATS (COCONUT OIL AND PALM OIL)
  ~ Contain many short fatty acids (risk of saponification!)
  ~ Pleasant feeling in the mouth (not fatty)
  ~ Melt easily (fresh)
  ~ Very poor compatibility of fats with long fatty acids (cocoa butter)

FATS WITH LONG AND MODERATELY SATURATED FATTY
ACIDS
  ~ Moderately saturated: cocoa butter and CBE
  ~ Have a simple composition
  ~ Very complex crystallisation
  ~ Pleasant melting behaviour just below body temper-
    ature
  ~ Short melting path
  ~ Good hardness

FATS WITH LONG AND HEAVILY UNSATURATED FATTY
ACIDS
  ~ Heavily unsaturated: all nut oils (hazelnut, almond,
    cashew, macadamia, brazil), soybean, sunflower oil,
    coleseed oil, etc.
  ~ Very low melting paths, hence liquid at low tempera-
    tures 0°C (32°F)
  ~ Sensitive to oxidation
  ~ When mixed with cocoa butter they reduce hardness

MILK FAT
- ~ Very complex animal fat with all kinds of possible fatty acids
- ~ Very long melting path 0-40°C (32-104°F)
- ~ Sensitive to saponification
- ~ Bad crystallisation
- ~ Has a very negative effect on the crystallisation behaviour of cocoa butter. Witness the difference in hardness between dark chocolate (cocoa butter only) and milk chocolate (cocoa butter and milk fat)

PARTIALLY HYDROGENATED FATS (LONG FATTY ACIDS)
- ~ Broad melting behaviour, is therefore popular for centre fats
- ~ Bad crystallisation
- ~ Rather poor compatibility with cocoa butter
- ~ Migration of these fats will soften the chocolate shell and can cause fat bloom

HYDROGENATED FATS (LAURIC FATS SUCH AS COCONUT AND PALM NUT)
- ~ Short melting path, used in compound coatings
- ~ Very fast crystallisation
- ~ Good snap
- ~ Not compatible when mixed with cocoa butter

Sugars

SUCROSE (SUGAR) / **Has strong sweetening power (100) and provides robust texture.** Extends shelf life. Typically crystallises (graining) when oversaturated. Lowers Aw value. Not soluble in alcohol. Lowers the product's cost price. Provides aroma and colour when caramelised.

GLUCOSE SYRUP / **Inhibits and slows down crystallisation.** Lowers Aw value. Provides aroma and colour when heated. Mostly used at:
- ~ 43° Baumé = 80% solid
- ~ 45° Baumé = 85% solid

Sweetening power:
- ~ glucose 60 DE (= 65)[4]
- ~ glucose 38 DE (= 45)
- ~ glucose 30 DE (= 30)

Works hygroscopically[5] (especially with high DE).

Low-DE glucose increases viscosity. Low-DE glucose serves as a thickener and strengthens (for example, a low fat ganache structure).

Glucose with low DE (< 40%) contains few reducing sugars, but many higher sugars and is recommended for hard drops, caramels, nougat, etc., because this quality has low hygroscopy and prevents transformation in cold temperatures.

Glucose with high DE (> 45%) is mostly used for items that contain a lot of water, such as marshmallows, since in this case water-thickening characteristics of reducing sugars slow down drying

DEXTROSE (GRAPE SUGAR) / **Sweetening power (30).** Ideal for lowering the sweetening effect on centres. Dissolves relatively disappointingly. Inhibits crystallisation in creams. Decreases the average crystal dimensions of the added sugars and provides some flexibility, which can be useful in preparations such as fondant sugar. Has "cooling" effect in the mouth (monohydrate only). Lowers Aw value. Is very hygroscopic.

INVERT SUGAR / **Sweetening power (125).** Contains 50% dextrose + 50% fructose (solid). Inhibits crystallisation in creams. Lowers Aw value if not heated over 70°C (158°F). Is hygroscopic. Is a desirable ingredient in items with high water content, which must be kept soft. An excess of inverted sugar can lead to stickiness and syrup secretion. Usually up to 25% will yield a good result. When heated provides aroma and colour.

INVERTASE / **Is marketed under various brand names.** This enzyme is able to split sucrose into its two components, i.e. the simple reducing sugars glucose and fructose (= invert sugar). Is mostly used to make specific centres softer by inverting the sugar. Most of the inverting takes place within seven days (alcohol can slow down the effect). Use 2 to 5 g per 1,000 g. It Best added between 60 and 70°C (140-158°F). The pH value must be between 3.8 and 5.2. Temperatures over 70°C (158°F) and high acid content destroy the effect of the invertase. Decreases viscosity. Its inverting effect provides a preserving quality (lowers Aw value). Must be kept cool and in a dark place. Its use is regulated in some countries.

HONEY / **Its composition varies depending on the plant variety, but on average consists of:**
- 18% water
- 38% fruit sugar (fructose): invert sugars
- 31% grape sugar (glucose): invert sugars
- 10% multiple sugars, minerals, organic acids and vitamins.
- 3% enzymes (or ferments), hormones, gluconic acid, colourings and flavourings.

Honey gives a characteristic flavour to a product. Because honey contains micro-organisms, it can be sensitive to fermentation in some centres. From a technical point of view the comments on invert sugar are also applicable here.

FRUCTOSE (FRUIT SUGAR) OR LAEVULOSE / **Sweetening power 130.** Inhibits crystallisation. Very soluble. Greatly lowers Aw value. If fruit flavour is added, the fruit taste increases. Very hygroscopic. Is very temperature sensitive (caramel).

LACTOSE / **Sweetening power 27.** Crystallises finely. Lowers Aw value. Sets the aromas.

SORBITOL (E420) / **Occurs naturally in a great variety of ripe fruits: apples, pears, grapes, some other berries and seaweed.** Quantity 5-10%. If the quantity is more than 5%, an equal amount of glucose syrup should be removed from the recipe. Its use is regulated in some countries. Exists in two forms:
- powder
- concentrate (70% solids)

Sweetening power 50. Inhibits crystallisation. Has a preserving and stabilising effect. Lowers Aw value. Is hygroscopic. Is a limited moisture stabiliser, and prevents drying. Has a cooling effect on the tongue. Tolerates high temperatures, however, between 150-170°C (302-338°F) colouring occurs (brown). Is very stable for acids, enzymes and temperatures up to 140°C (248°F).

Other sweeteners

NATURAL /

FRUITS
many fruits contain sugar (often fructose). Pureed fruits can be included in a recipe. For example in fruit jelly, fruit dough and even in ganaches. (Some superficial aromas can disappear in the process.)

MAPLE SYRUP
sap from the (Canadian) maple tree. The sap contains approximately 34% water and 66% sugar.

PALM SUGAR
dark, sticky sugar with many flavourings. This sugar is extracted from palm trees. Each palm variety has its own flavour. Gula aren is the sap of aren- or sugar palm trees.

CAROB FLOUR
see section on "Characteristics of the most frequently used ingredients". Sweetening power: 0.50-0.60.

GULA DJAWA
mixture of cane and palm sugar. After reducing, the sap is crystallised in a mould. Gula djawa has a very distinctive, spicy flavour and is used frequently in Indonesian cooking.

DATE SYRUP

is made from very sugar-rich dates. It is a dark syrup with a free neutral taste.

JAGGERY

unrefined or semi-refined sugar from dates. Has a distinct strong caramel taste.

MANNA SUGAR

sap from the manna ash, a 6 to 8 metre high tree, which grows mainly in Sicily and Southern Europe. The air-dried sap flows from abrasions in the trunk and boughs.

AGAVE SYRUP

sweetening power is higher than for saccharose. Contains 23-25% water. The agave is cultivated in Mexico. The syrup is then extracted in accordance with a patented and totally natural process from organically grown agave plants (blue agave).

STEVIA

from the stevia plant. Is twice as sweet as saccharose.

SUGAR SUBSTITUTES /   The following product summary is for information only. If used, they should be applied with the required knowledge and in minimum quantities.

INULIN

Is collected by extraction with warm water from the chicory root and is 100% organic. While inulin is a sugar, it does not have a sweet flavour. This white creamy substance is an ideal fat substitute and bulking agent. Inulin is calorie-reducing and is considered a fibre. Is mostly used together with a sugar substitute and/or sweetener.

POLYDEXTROSE (E1201)

Fat substitute and bulking agent.

SUGAR ALCOHOLS /

MANNITOL

A natural sweetener occurring in all kinds of vegetables. Has a light sweet flavour, with no aftertaste. 0.6 times as sweet as sugar. Daily use should not exceed 15 g (laxative!).

XYLITOL

A natural sweetener occurring in all kinds of vegetables and fruit varieties. Is just as sweet as saccharose. Has a sweet flavour, with no aftertaste. Daily use should not exceed 20 g (laxative!).

ISOMALT

A bulk sweetener[6]. Has a generous natural sweetness (0.45). Is the only sugar substitute exclusively extracted from sugar beet. Isomalt has a number of special characteristics. It is suitable for diabetics and is not hygroscopic (it therefore gives some recipes a longer shelf life).
Does not lead to Maillard reaction[7]. Since the sweetening power of isomalt is only half that of saccharose, it is mostly used combined with intense sweeteners such as acesulfame-K.

MALTITOL

A bulk sweetener. Is produced by hydrogenising maltose (starch). Sweetening power is somewhat lower than that of saccharose (= 0.9 times).Temperature stability.

LACTITOL

An artificial sweetener. Is made from milk sugar (lactose) and hydrogenation. Is 0.4 times as sweet as saccharose and has a sugary flavour, with no aftertaste.

ARTIFICIAL SWEETENERS /   Some artificial sweeteners do not have enough sweetening power, so that extra sweeteners need to be added. Large doses of sugar alcohols work as a laxative and can lead to serious health complaints.

ACESULFAME-K

Is a bulk sweetener, man made and 200 times sweeter than sugar. Heat-resistant up to 225°C (437°F) and therefore the first sweetener suitable for use in baking and cooking.

CYCLAMATE

Artificial sweetener. 30 times sweeter than saccharose.

SACCHARIN
Artificial sweetener. 300 to 500 times sweeter than saccharose.

ASPERTAME
Artificial sweetener. 200 times sweeter than saccharose. Its chemical composition is often considered
harmful to the human body. Products sweetened with
aspartame must be labelled with the warning "contains
a source of phenylalanine".

Additives

GLYCERINE (GLYCEROL) (E422) / Colourless and
odourless liquid (sweetening power 60). Low energy
sweetener soluble in water and not poisonous. Produced from sugars through fermentation. Hydrolysis
of animal or vegetable fat is also a source. Preservative
as it counters the loss of moisture. Greatly decreases Aw
(small molecules hence more molecules for the same
weight than, for example, Sorbitol). Used to counter
the drying out of pastry and fillings, to improve shine
and as a softener. Does not crystallise. 'Quatum satis'
quantity, i.e., the measurement necessary to achieve
the desired effect.

LECITHIN (E322) /   Is an emulsifier (combines with fat
to form an emulsion with water). Principal characteristics: Increases the lubricating effect of fats and decreases the surface tension. Ideal for lowering viscosity
in items such as chocolate and nut centres.
Optimal effect takes place by adding 0.5%. Adding
more has opposite effect. If more than 0.7% is added,
viscosity increases.
The effect of lecithin lessens considerably above 80°C.
Egg yolks are the richest source of lecithin (6 to 7%),
but it is also found in vegetable oils from rapeseed, sunflower seeds and maize. Its main industrial source is the
soybean (1.5 to 2%). Lecithin is practically tasteless and
odourless

Thickening and whipping agents

PECTIN (E440) /   Natural thickener formed from the
residue of apples and citrus fruits. Apple pectin solutions are clear, those of citrus fruits opaque. There is
little difference between the thickening power of the
two varieties.
The quantity of pectin to be used depends on the pH
value of the centre and that is why it is mostly recommended for thickening fruit dough and jams. Pectin
has its best thickening power at a value of pH 3-4. Used
frequently in jams and jellies. The gum is used in
marshmallows to stabilise the foam, in caramels the fat
is emulsified. Stabilising effect in beverages and ice
cream.

GELATINE /   This thickener is used very little in chocolate products. Gelatine contains 84 to 90% protein,
which makes it a good whipping agent for nougat,
mousses and marshmallows. Since gelatine is considered more of an ingredient than an additive, it does not
carry an E-number.
Because of its origins gelatine cannot be used by Jews
or Muslims. Gelatine softens and swells in cold water,
melts above 40°C (104°F) and gelatinises when cooled.
Gelatine is very heat-sensitive. Above 60°C (140°F) the
product loses its gelatinising power. On direct contact
with a heat source it scorches rapidly.
The quality of gelatine is expressed in "bloom" (mostly
between 50 and 300). This indicates the jelly strength.

AGAR-AGAR OR GELOSE (E406)* /   Thickener and gelling agent, derived from seaweed. Comes in bars and
in powdered form. In small quantities agar-agar has
greater thickening power than gelatine. 1 g agar-agar
can be used as a substitute for 3 g gelatine.
Swells in cold water and melts above 85°C (185°F). 1% in
syrup is sufficient to gelatinise when cooled at
30°C(86°F). Swells less in an acid environment. Has a
low Kcal value. Is primarily used for fruit jellies, jams,
marshmallows and all manner of creams. Warning!
Consult your legislation as there are national limits.

CARRAGEEN (E407)* /   Thickening and gelling agent
and, as with agar-agar, derived from seaweed (Chon-
drus crispus). Does not swell easily in cold water. Is

tasteless. Is primarily used in jellies, milk products and creams to increase viscosity in liquids, produce and stabilise emulsions. Warning! Consult your legislation as there are national limits.

GUAR GUM (E412)* / **Thickening agent and stabiliser.** Does well in cold water. Very stable at various pH values. Warning! Consult your legislation as there are national limits.

CAROB (ST. JOHN'S BREAD)* / **Beans from the carob tree (grows in the Mediterranean area and in West Asia).** The beans are ground into flour. The flour con-tains 50-60% sugar and can therefore be used as a sugar substitute in specific cases. Is very rich in calcium, and contains some fat and other substances.
Is used as a cocoa substitute in compound coating for people with cocoa allergies. The beans have a flavour that is roughly comparable to cocoa. The technical aspects of carob are comparable to cocoa.

CAROB GUM (E410)* / **In addition to the beans, the resin is also used as a thickener and stabiliser.** Has the same characteristics as guar gum. Mixes well with water and is a good stabiliser.

GUM ARABIC (E414)* / **Hardened sap of acacia tree.** Available in chunks, powder, sterilised and freeze dried. Thickening agent, emulsifier and stabiliser. Gum Arabic is stable in an acid environment and is used frequently as an emulsifier in the production of concentrated essential cola and citrus oils for use in soft drinks.

Used as foam stabiliser in some drinks. Prevents crystallising and fat deposition in sugar products. In ice cream, undesirable formation of large crystals can be better monitored.

Gum Arabic can best be dissolved by soaking it in its own weight in warm water overnight.

STARCH (AMYLUM) / **Important thickening agent for baked products and puddings.** Starches are not absorbed well in cold water and swell when heated. Is used very little in the chocolate industry, as it quickly loses its stability in moist environments.

Maltodextrins: dextrin or maltodextrins are starch derivatives. They are produced in the same way as glucose, through enzymatic or acid hydrolysis. White to pale powder soluble in water. Sweetening power: 10-30 Have a strong anti-crystallising and thickening effect, and as a result can partially replace the gum Arabic in hard gums.

Because of their viscosity they strengthen the gelatinising power. This stabilising role can be used in lightly beaten products to stabilise the foam structure. Slight discolouration in Maillard reaction.

ALGINATES (E400-E405)* / **Alginates are vegetable gums.** Very active thickeners, stabilisers and gelling agents. In concentrations of 0.25-0.5% they improve the stability of centres for baked goods, chocolate milk and ice cream. In ice cream, prevents the formation of undesirable large crystals.

Whipping agents

A large number of ingredients have the property of retaining the air that is mechanically injected, through the uniform dispersion of air bubbles. This makes centres lighter and changes their texture.

Whipping agents must meet certain requirements:
- Be soluble in water and sugar solutions
- Must function in broad pH environment
- Must be able to render airy rather concentrated sugar syrup
- Must keep its capacity, even in variable temperatures

Several proteins have this whipping capacity (egg albumin, gelatine, modified soy protein, ethyl- methyl cellulose, whey and low fat milk powder).

HYFOAMA DS / **Natural, heat-resistant whipping agent based on milk proteins.** Is used to partially or completely replace egg whites in chocolate products. See www.questintl.com

FRAPPE / **Is a ready made whipping agent.** Mostly consists of vegetable proteins or soy. Available on the market under several brand names. Is used to improve the structure and consistency of creams, centres, marshmallows, nougat, caramels and fondant cream centres. Is also often used to make them cheaper. Can easily be home made. For recipe, see "Miscellaneous - Frappe" section.

SODIUM BICARBONATE (BICARBONATE OF SODA) / **Acidity regulator.** Used frequently when fruits are processed in recipes in order to neutralise acidity. It is preferable to bring the fruits in contact with the sodium bicarbonate first. Makes sweet creams appear less sweet.

TARTAR (POTASSIUM BITARTRATE) / **known by its scientific name "cremor tartari".** Used as replacement for glucose in sugar recipes. Has a shorter structure than glucose in sugar items. Is often used to stabilise beaten egg white. Tartar is not very soluble in cold water. Dosage is approximately 0.1% and is added to sugar syrup after it has reached its saturation point, 105-110°C (221-230°F), to slow down crystallisation.

TARTARIC ACID (E334) / **Is an acidifier.** Is sometimes used as a replacement for citric acid. Is derived from pressed grape residue in wine production. Tartaric acid is soluble in water. 70 g tartaric acid has the same effect as 100 g citric acid.

CITRIC ACID (E330) / **Citric acid provides a softer acid flavour than tartaric acid.** It is produced from crushed lemon and other acid fruit crystals, or by fermenting sugar solutions in the presence of specific micro-organisms. Strengthens the flavour of fruit dough. Easily soluble in water and alcohol.

SORBIC ACID (E200)* / **Sorbic acid is a preservative.** Works best in centres with a maximum of 4-5 pH. Slows down fermentation and fungi in centres with high water concentration. Is not very effective against bacteria. Do not add more than 0.1% of the total recipe (risk of taste detection).

POTASSIUM SORBATE (E202)* / **Preservative, same as sorbic acid.**

BENZOIC ACID (E210)* / **Preservative.** Very effective against fermentation and fungi, average effect on bacteria.

Spice mixtures

Ready made spice mixtures, available on the market:
- Spice mixtures for gingerbread mostly consist of cinnamon, orange rind, coriander, ginger, anise, cloves, cardamom and nutmeg.
- Mixed spice: 270 g cinnamon, 75 g nutmeg, 75 g cloves, 60 g ginger, 30 g cardamom and 20 g pepper.
- Four spice: cinnamon, cloves, nutmeg, ginger.
- Five spice: cinnamon, cloves, nutmeg, pepper, Jamaican pepper.

Flavours

The traditional flavours that have dominated our palate for a long time – coffee, vanilla, cinnamon, and all kinds of liqueurs – have recently had to share their position in the market with new trends such as herbal infusions, dried and ground spices, and previously little known, or unknown, plants. Quite a few spices and plants that are currently conquering our markets, were unknown to us before because they came from faraway countries. These new products challenge us to experiment and create subtle blends. Developing and combining new flavours and aromas is above all about "doing" and "daring", and yet some expertise is required. The combination of flavours and ingredients can, depending on the ingredient, have different effects. Some recipes are 'over the top', whereby many different ingredients are often needlessly mixed. This is no guarantee for a fine and delicious tasting experience. As the old saying goes: "Restraint is proof of true greatness" ... meaning that exaggeration misses its target

Aromas not only serve as a basis for reproducing specific flavours, they can also be used to strengthen or enhance other flavours.

SOME EXAMPLES /
- A touch of anise makes whipped cream taste and smell of fresh cream from the farm.
- Ginger softens flavours, and smoothes out rough edges. Add a hint of red peppers and ginger to a ganache.
- A dash of rose flavouring (Rose oil extract 526, by Amoretti) added to marzipan, in combination with sweet fruits such as dates and figs, balances the blend.
- Adding raspberries to cranberries, will enhance the cranberry flavour.
- Adding pineapple can enhance cherries, apples and pears.
- A little apricot extract enhances the flavour of peaches and apricots.
- Raspberries and strawberries improve each other's flavours. By adding a little raspberry spirit to strawberries, or strawberry spirit to raspberries, the fruit flavour is enhanced.
- A good dash of raspberry vinegar in water is a cure for strawberries with little flavour (allow to absorb for ten minutes or so).
- Adding a little balsamic vinegar to strawberry puree, boosts the strawberry aroma.
- A splash of gin enhances the main flavour of many creams.
- Strawberries, raspberries and cherries lose their own unique flavour if processed together. Add a hint of vanilla ... and strawberry, raspberry and cherry flavours can again be distinguished.

THE ART IS TO COMBINE TASTES IN A SUBTLE MANNER TO OBTAIN A HARMONIOUS CREATION / **If sciences were ranked according to their degree of difficulty, physics would no doubt be the easiest.** Biology and life sciences would be the most difficult. Sensory research is a combination of the last two and is, therefore, very difficult to implement, as humans are used as measuring instruments. Measuring instruments can be calibrated, but man's sense of taste cannot.

This is why as many external factors as possible must be neutralised to prevent them from influencing the tasting process and to obtain accurate taste results. When we taste something that is nicely packaged in a sufficiently lit environment, accompanied by a good narrative, our judgement will generally be positive. The reverse is also true: no matter how tasty the finished product, if we taste it in a dark, noisy environment, packaged in plain colourless wrapping, our attitude will be negative before we have tasted it.

Objectivity is, therefore, the most important attribute of a good taster.

[1] Couverture:chocolate coating, this name only exists in the EU.

[2] Fat migration: See section on "Shelf life". "Fat bloom".

[3] Cocoa Butter Equivalent.

[4] DE = Dextrose Equivalent (percentage reducing sugar calculated on solid).

[5] Hygroscopic: attracts moisture from the air.

[6] Bulk sweeteners: per unit of weight have a sweetening power just below, or comparable to, that of sugar (e.g., maltitol, xylitol, lactitol, sorbitol).

Intensive sweeteners are sweeteners of which the sweetening power per unit of weight is considerably greater than that of sugar (e.g., saccharin, cyclamates, acesulfame-K and aspartame).

[7] Maillard reaction: See section on "Caramelising".

[8] E-number: only important in EU countries. Other countries just use the name of the additive.

[*] Warning! Consult your legislation as there are national limits.

Chocolate processing

Precrystallising *33* / Time – movement – temperature zone *33* /
Over-crystallising and under-crystallising *37* / Tempermeter *38* / Cooling *39* /
Undesirable defects – what can be done? *40* /

Precrystallising

Precrystallising is the preparation process of bringing chocolate to its correct crystalline form. It replaces the old-fashioned concept of "tempering", which was erroneously interpreted by many an expert, since the chocolate was brought to a specific processing temperature. This way the chocolate did not always achieve the desired result, despite the fact that the correct temperature was aimed for.

Correct temperature does not mean that the correct crystalline form is present. But if the correct crystalline form is present, the chocolate is in a specific temperature zone. It is logical for beginners who are only focused on temperature, to achieve uncertain results.

For optimum results melted chocolate must be precrystallised. Precrystallising means that the required number of seed crystals are produced in the chocolate. Succesfully precrystallised chocolate provides the end product with the following desirable properties:

- ~ Gloss
- ~ Hardness
- ~ Good shrinkage
- ~ Release of aroma
- ~ Smooth in the mouth
- ~ Longer shelf life
- ~ Good snap

Incorrect (or insufficient) precrystallised chocolate presents the following disadvantages:

- ~ Lack of sheen
- ~ Grey/white colouring
- ~ Sensitive to the touch (melts quickly when touched)
- ~ No shrinkage
- ~ Grainy structure
- ~ Quickly develops fatbloom

WHY PRECRYSTALLISING? / **The presence of cocoa butter is the reason why chocolate is precrystallised.** In contrast to many other fats, cocoa butter needs to be a polymorph[1], which means that it can crystallise in different crystalline forms. It is generally accepted that cocoa butter can display six different crystalline forms, each with a specific melt temperature: γ (gamma), α (alpha), β" (beta double), β' (beta prime), β (beta) and Form VI. Only the β form gives chocolate its good qualities. The desired properties are determined by properly processing the cocoa butter.

Form VI is the most stable form, but has too high a melt temperature.

The others are unstable. They have a lower melt temperature and tend to transform into a more stable form over time, which translates into grey/white specks.

The melt temperatures of the principal crystalline forms are:

γ	melt temperature at	16°C	(60,8°F)
α		22°C	(70°F)
β'		28°C	(82,4°F)
β		34°C	(93,2°F)
Form VI		36°C	(96,8°F)

Names can be displayed differently in other sources, also Form VI, which is still not widely known.

For optimum gloss, shrinkage and hardness the cocoa butter must be brought to the stable beta form. Actually, 0.1 to 0.2% beta crystals suffice for full crystallisation of the quantity of cocoa butter. It is important to know that the four first crystalline forms only appear in liquid chocolate, whilst the sixth form, at a later time, appears like a white film on the product. (This "ageing" process can occur after only one week and up to one year or longer.) This is why it is very important that only stable crystals be formed in the solidifying chocolate, to harden rapidly and produce an attractive glossy product.

Time – movement – temperature zone

MELTING / **Before the chocolate can be precrystallised, it must be melted.** The chocolate must never come in contact with a heat source, to prevent it from scorching. It is recommended that chocolate be melted between 40°C (104°F) and 45°C (113°F).

- ~ < 40°C (104°F) is not recommended, as unmelted seeds could be left, which could give the precrystallised chocolate unusual viscosity during processing.
- ~ > 50°C (122°F) and up to 55°C (131°F) represents a risk of scorching.

PRECRYSTALLISING / **There are various methods of precrystallising chocolate.** Some are better or not as good as others, depending on the options and working conditions.

The aim is to bring the cacao butter in the chocolate to its most correct β crystalline form. All methods have the same aim – creating stable crystals – and require the same parameters to be able to create these stable crystals: Time – movement – temperature zone

When a bowl of melted chocolate cools straight away, the chocolate will begin to solidify after a very long time, and the temperature will have decreased. However, the chocolate looks grainy and grey.

If the bowl is stirred regularly (movement), the chocolate will solidify much more rapidly, and the correct crystal structure will be obtained, which yields an attractive end result. In the second example, three elements played a role: time, temperature and movement.

FIRST METHOD (GRAPH 1)

The tabliering method on marble is a classic but old-fashioned method. This method is used very little nowadays as it is too time-consuming and less hygienic.

- Pour approximately 2/3 of the melted chocolate onto a marble surface.

Spread out the mass and work it (movement) with a spatula until after some time the chocolate reaches a temperature at which it thickens slightly. This quantity includes a profusion of seed crystals and should be added to the reserved warm chocolate as quickly as possible. This slightly raises the temperature and the unstable crystals, which are also created on the marble surface, are melted again or retransformed into more stable crystalline forms.

- In theory the initial temperature for dark chocolate should not exceed 32°C (89.6°F). Because of the existing milkfat in milk and white chocolate, the initial temperature for milk chocolate should not exceed 30°C (86°F) and for white chocolate 28-29°C (82.4-84.2°F).

- If not enough seed crystals were formed in the 2/3 portion (due to insufficient cooling) or if 1/3 was still too warm, all the seed crystals created on the marble are melted out and a portion of the chocolate will be cooled again on the marble surface.

SECOND METHOD (GRAPH 2)

This method takes a long time, but requires little effort.

- The melted chocolate just cools down until the mass starts solidifying (time). A great many stable crystals were created.

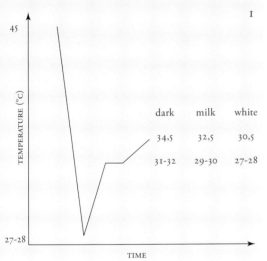

	dark	milk	white
	34,5	32,5	30,5
	31-32	29-30	27-28

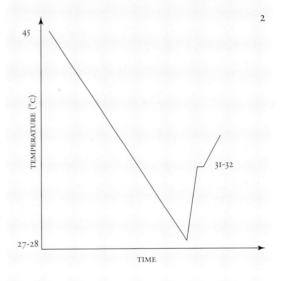

- While constantly stirring (movement) the chocolate is heated until the mass reaches its initial temperature. By slightly raising the temperature, the excess crystals melt out.

THIRD METHOD (GRAPH 3)
Since the bought chocolate chunks are stably crystallised, the excess stable crystals that have turned the chocolate into a solid mass can be melted out, by means of a very slow melting process. To this end a heating chamber or incubator with a very precise thermostat is required.

- The chunks are preferably placed in the heat chamber or incubator the previous day (time).
- The thermostat is set (temperature): For dark chocolate at 34-35°C (93.2-95°F), for milk chocolate at 32-33°C (89.6-91.4°F), for white chocolate 31-32°C (87.8-89.6°F) .
- If the chocolate is still a little too thick the next morning, it shows that there are still too many seed

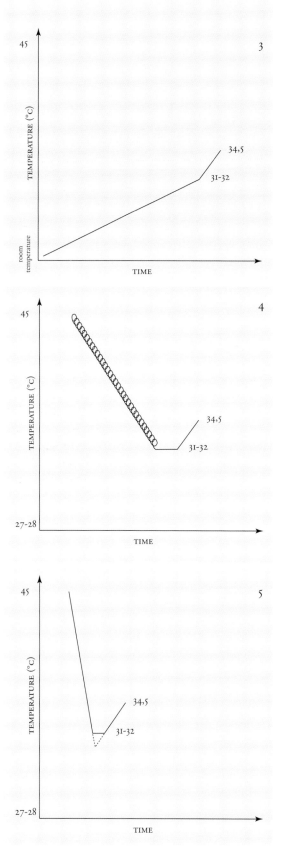

crystals present (over/crystallisation[2]). In this case the mass will be slightly heated while being stirred (movement), until the correct viscosity is achieved.

- If the mass is more liquid than in normally precrystallised chocolate, the melt temperature was too high, which caused all stable crystals to melt. In the future the melt temperature will be slightly lowered.

FOURTH METHOD (GRAPH 4)

Only applicable to industrial production or to very small quantities of chocolate.

- The melted chocolate is cooled under constant stirring (movement) until it reaches its initial temperature. A certain cooling time is therefore required. With this method there is no undercooling, which has the important advantage that no unstable crystals are created.

FIFTH METHOD (GRAPH 5)

The fastest and easiest method is the seed method. Hard chocolate contains an enormous amount of stable crystals and is therefore appropriate for first lowering the temperature, and then to be used as seeds. This working method is very suitable since no work takes place in the zone in which unstable crystals are formed.

- Break chocolate into small chunks or use chocolate drops.

The chocolate chunks are just about at room temperature and will soon lower the temperature of the melted chocolate by 40-45°C (104-113°F), but as they do so they melt out.

- If the initial temperature of the chocolate is reached and all chunks have been easily melted, this shows that all stable crystals that were present in the hard chocolate, were probably also melted out. Add some more chunks; they do not melt that easily. The added quantity depends on the temperature of the chocolate. The warmer the temperature, the more chocolate chunks are added.

USE OF MICROWAVE OVEN

Melting chocolate in a microwave oven is consistent with the third method.

A microwave oven can be a good aid for melting or precrystallising a small quantity of chocolate in a very short time.

It is indeed possible to create a precrystallised mass from hard chocolate, within a very short time.

- Very important: Heat the chocolate during limited periods on reduced power and stir regularly.
- When the chocolate starts to melt, it is important that enough stable crystals remain, so that the mass can be seeded.

Warning: If the chocolate is heated for too long on high power, there is a risk of scorching.

Over-crystallising and under-crystallising

OVER-CRYSTALLISING / **Checking whether chocolate is correctly precrystallised, can happen very simply by placing a small quantity of chocolate on paper or on the tip of a knife.** If it is correctly precrystallised the chocolate will harden evenly within minutes and display an attractive gloss. From this moment on it is important to check the chocolate constantly for viscosity, since stable beta crystals will now start multiplying. This growth does not stop; on the contrary the process speeds up, which means that the chocolate will slowly start to thicken.

If at this time the chocolate is processed further, despite the correct processing temperature, the shell will get thicker, air bubbles will be created, there will be less gloss (bloom may even appear) and with moulded shapes less shrinkage. There are too many stable crystals, which will release more crystallisation heat, and hence faster cooling is required to divert this heat. Slow cooling will give the chocolate a coarse crystal structure, which will lead to increased risk of bloom.

Conclusion: slow down the multiplication of crystals and try to constantly work with the same number of crystals!

A thermometer is of no use in this case! Attention must be paid that the same attractive viscosity is maintained, as obtained after precrystallisation. This can happen two ways:

- When slight thickening occurs, the chocolate temperature is somewhat increased, in order for all new crystals to bc constantly melted out and for the same number of crystals to be maintained. This increase in temperature should be implemented very gradually in order not to melt out too many crystals. Start with 0.5°C (0.9°F). If the chocolate keeps on thickening, increase by another 0.5°C (0.9°F) until the correct viscosity is reached again. It can now stay even for a long time, until suddenly, despite a higher working temperature, the chocolate once again has a tendency to thicken. The temperature can be slowly increased to 34.5°C (94.1°F) for dark chocolate, 32.5°C (90.5°F) for milk chocolate and 30.5°C (86.9°F) for white chocolate, depending on the recipe (quantity of cocoa butter/butter oil).
- Another option to maintain the correct quantity of stable crystals is to regularly add small quantities of melted non-precrystallised chocolate, to the precrystallised chocolate. Under no circumstances should cocoa butter be added!

UNDER-CRYSTALLISING / **If the chocolate is thinner and more liquid than usual after precrystallisation, this means that during precrystallisation too few (or no) stable crystals were produced.** This is a case of under crystallised chocolate. Even though the chocolate has a perfect processing temperature, it has a granular texture or shows fatbloom after hardening.

- If the chocolate still hardens after a short time, but shows little or no gloss, it is sufficient to add stable crystals by stirring over a longer period. More time and more movement.
- If the chocolate does not harden within five minutes, there are no stable crystals, and further precrystallisation is required.

Tempermeter

PRINCIPLE
a tempermeter is a kind of rudimentary calorimeter[3]. It shows how chocolate is precrystallised from a temperature/time curve.

APPARATUS
- Copper test tube
- Cooling element (melting ice or electronic element)
- Recording thermometer

OPERATION
A constant quantity of precrystallised chocolate is placed in the upper section of the copper tube, the lower section of the tube is placed in the cooling element. A lid is placed on the upper section containing a temperature sensor dipped in the chocolate. The temperature is recorded during cooling.
During crystallisation of the chocolate crystallisation heat is released. This results in a more or less S-shaped curve on the temperature recording. Depending on precrystallisation, the crystallisation heat is released at a lower or higher speed and whereby the S-shape changes. The precrystallisation degree can be read with a template using this result.

USE
Primarily for industrial applications.
The accuracy, and particularly the consistency, of precrystallisation can be controlled for identical chocolates and applications. Depending on for example the fat composition (cacao butter/milk fat ratio) the ideal tempering curve will vary. Different applications may require different kinds of precrystallised chocolate.

Cooling

Chocolate that is not cooled properly despite perfect precrystallisation can turn dull or grey.

As soon as the pralines are made and the chocolate starts to solidify (crystals keep on multiplying until the chocolate is fully hardened), the crystallisation process runs exothermically[1]. This crystallisation heat must be correctly transferred, as the cooling method is of the utmost importance for the end result. If the heat is not transferred in time, the crystallisation process will take place too slowly, resulting in coarse crystals being formed, which turn the chocolate (from the inside out) grey/white.

There is a difference between moulded and dull products.

MOULDED PRODUCTS / **Since the chocolate is isolated by the mould, rapid cooling is a must.** In order to avoid condensation moisture[5], the chocolate should not be subjected to excessive temperature changes. The refrigerator temperature should ideally be approximately 10°C (18°F) lower than the ambient temperature.

However, if the cooling space is filled with a great number of moulds simultaneously, it is of course possible that cooling will not occur quickly enough. Adjust the cooling temperature in this case.

A ventilated refrigerator is a must for chocolate work, as the crystallisation heat must be cancelled out by wind force.

Convection[6] is the most prevalent form of heat transfer in chocolate cooling, and can be very accurately adjusted by regulating the air speed. Usually air temperatures of 7°C (44.6°F) and air speeds of approximately 7 m/sec are applied. The thicker the chocolate layer, the faster the required cooling.

DULL PRODUCTS / **In contrast to moulded products the chocolate on dull products is in direct contact with the cooling medium.** This allows for less aggressive cooling, and the difference should be no greater than 9-10°C (16.2-18°F). Otherwise there is a risk of ending up in an unstable crystal zone, which causes loss of gloss, creates fat bloom and sensitivity to touch.

When using an enrober with a cooling tunnel, cooling by means of radiation is recommended. In this case, the temperature at the entrance to the tunnel should ideally be 18°C (64.4°F), in the middle 15°C (59°F) and at the exit of the tunnel approximately 18°C (64.4°F). The minimum transfer time should be 6 to 7 minutes, 10 to 12 minutes ideally. (It goes without saying that the quantity of products in the cooling tunnel also plays a role in the temperature setting.)

Warning: sometimes heat is only partially extracted from the chocolate around covered centres in so-called radiation tunnels. In general, heat transfer in these tunnels is rather slow and painstaking. Due to the air present in the tunnel mixed heat transfer can indeed take place here: by radiation and by convection.

The centres to be covered or dipped should not be cold. Excessive temperature changes are to be avoided, otherwise the chocolate will crystallise too quickly. Since unstable crystals are also formed, the chocolate coating may lose part of its gloss and appear dull. The best results are obtained when the temperature difference between centre and chocolate is less than 10°C (18°F).

Undesirable defects - what can be done?

UNDESIRABLE DEFECTS DURING MOULDING /

DULL PATCH OR LINE ON A NICE GLOSSY, EVEN SURFACE (PHOTO 1)
Possible cause
- The shrinking speed of chocolate is lower than that of the material of which the mould is made. This only occurs on smooth surfaces, with no unevenness in the mould. Typical defect in smooth Easter eggs. Does not occur in moulds with lots of detail.

Can be avoided by
- Using polycarbonate (Macrolon) moulds (where possible)
- Using appropriate chocolate. Chocolates with a high cocoa butter content have better shrinkage properties
- Using perfectly precrystallised chocolate with the correct amount of β crystals. Under- or over-crystallised chocolate has less shrinking power.
- Slightly preheating the moulds
- Allowing the chocolate to crystallise slowly (no sudden cooling)
- Cooling moulds that typically show dull patches for slightly longer periods

DULL (MAT) SURFACE OR LARGE DULL (MAT) PATCH (PHOTO 2)
Possible cause
- The chocolate was removed from the mould prematurely.
- Over-crystallised chocolate was used.

Can be avoided by
- Respecting cooling times. In clear moulds the chocolate's shrinking behaviour can be monitored from the outside. If dark patches persist, the mould requires further cooling.
- Using chocolate with the correct amount of β crystals.

AIR BUBBLES ON THE END PRODUCT (PHOTO 3)
Possible cause
- The chocolate is too thick for this application.
- The mould's edges or patterns are too sharp.

- The mould was not sufficiently vibrated.
Can be avoided by
- Using chocolate with a higher cocoa butter percentage.
- Not using over-crystallised chocolate. The excess β crystals must be melted out or some untempered chocolate must be added, so as to reduce the number of β crystals.

In the event of over-crystallisation: do not add cocoa butter (see section on "Over-crystallising").

DEMOULDING IS DIFFICULT DESPITE ATTRACTIVE GLOSS
Possible cause
- Shell too thin compared to mould dimensions. The chocolate cannot detach from the mould.
- Shell too thin for the mould. Conical moulds demould more easily than deep moulds with parallel sides.

Can be avoided by
- Using chocolate with viscosity suitable for these kinds of moulds.
- Filling the mould in two or three separate layers, depending on its dimensions. Each layer will be slightly crystallised, before the next layer is applied.

DOES NOT DEMOULD
Possible cause
- The chocolate is under-crystallised.
- The chocolate is over-crystallised.
- Insufficient cooling. Slow cooling creates coarse crystals, which limits the shrinking of the chocolate.

Can be avoided by
- Working with chocolate that contains the right amount of β crystals.
- Ensuring smooth but not overly rapid cooling.

CRACKS IN MOULDING
Possible cause
- Cooling to too low a temperature. The moulds were cooled to too low a temperature before the chocolate started to solidify.

1

2

3

4

5

6

7

8

9

- Shell too thin compared to mould dimensions

Can be avoided by

- Adjusting the cooling temperature (see section on "Cooling").
- First slightly solidifying the chocolate, before placing it in cooling.
- For some moulds, removing clamps after chocolate solidifies.

"RED" CHOCOLATE

Rare phenomenon.

Possible cause

- Chocolate is a little too hot.
- Mould is a little too hot.

Can be avoided by

- Seeding with extra β crystals and adjusting the temperature.

DIRTY MOULDS

Possible cause

- The chocolate is under-crystallised.
- The chocolate was poured into moulds that were too cold.
- As a result of a large temperature difference between cooling areas and workshop condensation occurred in the moulds.
- Soiling of moulds by centre.
- The moulds were handled on the inside.

Can be avoided by

- Using chocolate with the correct amount of β crystals.
- Slight preheating of moulds.
- Placing moulds in a cooling area in which the temperature is not too low (see section on "Cooling").
- Never touching the moulds on the inside with fingers.
- Washing and polishing moulds that are contaminated by fingerprints or centres.

UNDESIRABLE DEFECTS IN ENROBING (OR DIPPING) /

NO GLOSS ON ENROBING

Possible cause

- The chocolate is over-crystallised.
- The workshop is too cold.
- The centre is too cold.
- The cooling tunnel is at too low a temperature.

- Cooling tunnel is at too low a temperature whilst workshop temperature is warm. This causes sugar bloom.

Can be avoided by

- Using chocolate with the correct amount of β crystals.
- Working in an area with temperatures of at least 20°C (68°F).
- Ensuring that centre and chocolate temperatures are not too different. Otherwise the cold centre will have a negative influence on the crystallisation of the cocoa butter. This also produces a product that is mat and less resistant to heat.
- Ensuring cold products are not brought into a hot area, which would result in condensation on the coating. This causes sugar bloom after drying (see section on "Shelf life").

CHOCOLATE LAYER TOO THICK (PHOTO 4)

This results in the chocolate typically containing air bubbles.

Possible cause

- Unsuitable chocolate for this kind of work.
- Over-crystallised chocolate.

Can be avoided by

- Using a chocolate with a high cocoa butter content. (This yields an attractive thin chocolate shell during enrobing)
- Using chocolate with the correct amount of β crystals.
- (In manual work) sufficient patting of the chocolate surface. (As a result of the surface tension of the chocolate part of the chocolate is removed from the praline)
- (In mechanical enrobing) sufficient vibration of transport grid.
- (In mechanical enrobing) increasing strength of airflow system.

THE PRODUCTS HAVE ENLARGED BASES (PHOTO 5)

Possible cause

- Unsuitable chocolate for this kind of work.
- Slightly under-tempered chocolate.
- The recently covered products were moved too suddenly.

Can be avoided by
- Not using chocolate with too few β crystals, which causes the chocolate to be thin and liquid.
- First solidifying the chocolate and only then moving the products.

TRACES OF DIPPING FORK OR GRID AT THE BOTTOM OF THE PRALINES (PHOTO 6)
Possible cause
- The chocolate is too thick for this application.
- De pralines do not have a chocolate base.
Can be avoided by
- Applying a chocolate layer at the base of the flat plate before it is cut up with a wire slicer or knife.

AIR BUBBLES ON THE PRALINES (PHOTO 7)
Possible cause
- The chocolate is too thick for this application.
- Use of over-crystallised chocolate.
- Too little chocolate in the machine.
Can be avoided by
- Using chocolate with the correct amount of β crystals.
- Pouring a sufficient amount of chocolate into the machine. The enrober's pump or wheel blows air, which is absorbed by the chocolate.

UNDESIRABLE DEFECTS IN ENROBING AS WELL AS MOULDING /

FINGERPRINTS ON END PRODUCT
Possible cause
- The products have been touched with warm or moist fingers.
Can be avoided by
- Wearing gloves. (Not only for appearance, but also for reasons of hygiene.)

TURNING WHITE (WITHIN TWO DAYS AFTER PRODUCTION) (PHOTO 8)
Possible cause
- The chocolate is solidifying too slowly as the ambient temperature is too high.
- The products are not cooled.
- There was too long a delay before products were placed in cooling.
- Chocolate layer too thick.

For ways to avoid this
- See section on "Cooling".

GREY FILM AND ASPERITY WITH IRREGULAR DIMENSIONS
Possible cause
- The chocolate was not sufficiently precrystallised.
Can be avoided by
- Precrystallising the chocolate again, until it contains enough β crystals.

THICKENING OF CHOCOLATE DURING PROCESSING
Possible cause
- Over-crystallisation.
- The chocolate spent too much time in a moist environment.
For ways to avoid this
- See section on "Over-crystallising".

GREY OR MAT LINES ON THE CHOCOLATE (PHOTO 9)
Possible cause
- Since chocolate has an isolating effect, after heating chocolate will retain this heat locally. Therefore the chocolate has been badly mixed.
Can be avoided by
- Constantly stirring the chocolate, otherwise warm and cool layers are created. Warm layers will later turn into grey lines.

[1] Polymorphism: quality of a substance to crystallise in different forms (and dimensions).

[2] Over crystallisation: an excess of stable crystals. See the section "Over crystallising".

[3] Calorimeter: apparatus for measuring quantities of absorbed or emitted heat

[4] Exothermically: developing heat by physical or chemical process.

[5] Condensation moisture causes sugarbloom and gives the chocolate an old dull appearance.

[6] Convection: heat (or cold) is transferred by circulating hot air.

[7] Radiation: radiation does not need an intermediate medium and rays run in a straight line from one object to the other (i.e. sun radiating heat to the earth).

Rheology

Viscosity *45* / Yield value *45* / Chocolate application table *47* /

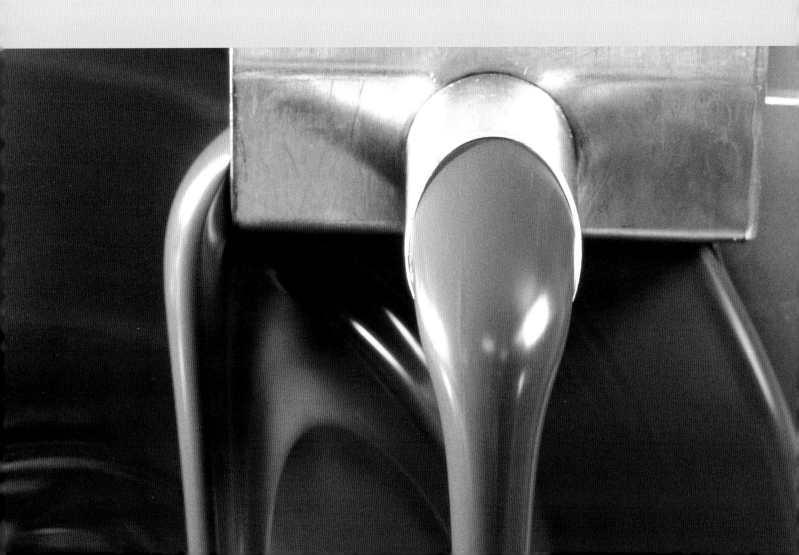

Rheology is the science that describes the flow behaviour of many products during processing (or in the end product). Rheology describes phenomena such as viscosity, yield value, elasticity, gel structure, etc.

In the context of this book viscosity and yield value are especially important characteristics in chocolate processing.

Viscosity

DEFINITION / **Viscosity describes the flow behaviour in terms of applied force.** Viscosity details provide us with a good idea of whether or not a chocolate will flow easily when processed (stirring, shaking, blowing).

VALUES / **Viscosity is expressed in Pa.s (Pascal-seconds) or mPa.s (millipascal-seconds).** A high number such as 7,000 mPa.s refers to very viscous chocolate. A low number such as 500 mPa.s refers to liquid chocolate.

INFLUENCE / **The viscosity of chocolate is influenced by the fat content and the emulsifiers present (lecithin).** Emulsifiers have been added in optimum doses by the chocolate manufacturer.

In practice the viscosity of chocolate can be lowered by adding cocoa butter (fat). (The chocolate gets thinner, more liquid).

Yield value

DEFINITION / **The yield value describes chocolate flow behaviour with minor applied forces, such as flowing under its own weight.**

VALUES / **The yield value is expressed in Pa (Pascal).** High values (30 Pa) refer to little or no flow. Low values (5 Pa) refer to strong flow.

INFLUENCE / **The fineness of the chocolate is especially important.** Very fine chocolate has a high yield value. Coarse chocolate has a low yield value. Very coarse chocolate has a very low yield value. The higher the fat content, the lower the yield value and viscosity.

Important: Using chocolate with an unadjusted yield value can result in defects on, and in, the end product.
- Sides that are too thin in mould pralines and enlarged bases in dipping are caused by an excessively low yield value.
- Irregular layer thickness in hollow goods is caused by too high a yield value.

Description	Extra thick	Very thick	Thick	Semi/liquid	Liquid	More liquid	Very liquid	Extra liquid	Very thin
Viscosity in mPa.s*	7000	4500	2500	1500	1000	700	500	300	150
Fat content in % **	25-27	28-29	30-32	33-35	35-38	38-39	39-41	41-45	60-65

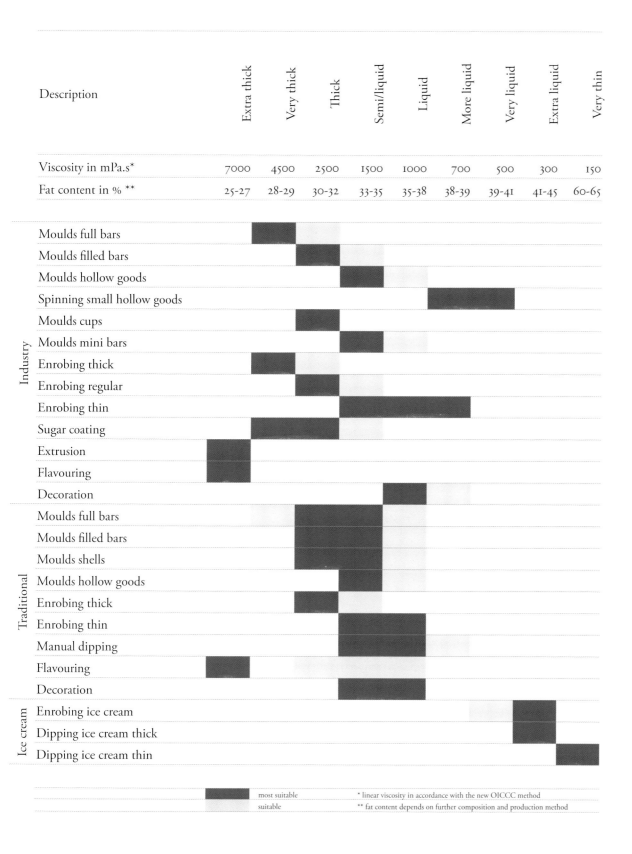

Industry
- Moulds full bars
- Moulds filled bars
- Moulds hollow goods
- Spinning small hollow goods
- Moulds cups
- Moulds mini bars
- Enrobing thick
- Enrobing regular
- Enrobing thin
- Sugar coating
- Extrusion
- Flavouring
- Decoration

Traditional
- Moulds full bars
- Moulds filled bars
- Moulds shells
- Moulds hollow goods
- Enrobing thick
- Enrobing thin
- Manual dipping
- Flavouring
- Decoration

Ice cream
- Enrobing ice cream
- Dipping ice cream thick
- Dipping ice cream thin

■ most suitable
■ suitable

* linear viscosity in accordance with the new OICCC method
** fat content depends on further composition and production method

04
Shelf life
and factors that extend shelf life

Environmental factors *49* / Migration *49* / Fat bloom *50* / Sugar bloom *50* /
Hygiene *52* / Factors that extend shelf life *52* / What can go wrong *53* /
What action to take *53* / Reduce water activity *53* /
Create a balance in relative humidity between centres and their environment *54* /
Add alcohol to the recipe *55* / Adjust acidity degree *55* /
Candying *55* / Cooling *55* / Freezing *55* / Drying *56* / Preservatives *56* /

Chocolate products are extremely sensitive to odours, air and light, humidity, vermin and temperature fluctuations.

Environmental factors

Odours / Chocolate easily absorbs external odours. This is why chocolate should be stored in an area that is free from musty or other irregular smells. Chocolate certainly should not be stored next to strong-smelling products (herbs, meat, fish, cheese, citrus fruits, etc.) The packaging material should also be completely odour-free. Smoking is strictly prohibited in areas where chocolate is kept.

LIGHT AND AIR / **Chocolate will oxidise more quickly and will be subject to significant flavour deviations when exposed to light and air.** This is why it is important to keep chocolate away from light (including artificial light) and air whenever possible and to store it in sealed packaging.
Dark chocolate and milk chocolate naturally contain a number of antioxidants (these are agents that slow down the oxidation process). White chocolate, however, does not contain these substances This is why white chocolate is much more sensitive to oxidation than dark or milk chocolate and white chocolate should, if possible, be given additional protection. The flavour changes as soon as there is an alteration in the colour (from yellow to white).

HUMIDITY / **Chocolate should be protected against humidity.** As a rule it should be stored in an area with a maximum relative humidity of 70%.

VERMIN / **The odour of chocolate can attract all kinds of vermin.**

TEMPERATURE FLUCTUATIONS / **The quality of chocolate products deteriorates faster under fluctuating storage temperatures (which accelerate the fat bloom phenomenon).** Constant temperature is an absolute must. The ideal temperature for storing chocolate is between 12 and 18°C (53.6-64.4°F). At higher temperatures the chocolate will soften and will lose its gloss.

Lower storage temperatures are less risky but when the products are brought back to room temperature, condensation should be avoided as this could result in sugar bloom. Bring the packaged chocolate to room temperature before opening the package.

Migration

In theory migration starts from the moment the chocolates are made until a kind of balance is achieved. If strong temperature fluctuations occur during storage, migration will actually never cease. Environmental conditions will always have an influence.
Migration cannot (yet) be avoided, but it can be slowed down, and almost always leads to a shorter shelf life. There is a difference between:
- moisture migration
- fat migration

MOISTURE MIGRATION / **Moisture migration can occur in products that have a high moisture content in the centre (fondant sugar, marzipan, foam centres, jellylike centres, soft caramel, etc.)** and leads to drying or hardening of the centre, or to the softening of a dry inclusion (such as Callebaut's pailleté feuilletine biscuits). The moisture in the centre can partially dissolve the sugar in the chocolate layer. Centres can also dry out. The moisture in the centre slowly evaporates through minuscule holes or tears in the chocolate layer. These tears are often created when the chocolate shrinks more than the centre when cooled.

FAT MIGRATION / **Fat migration occurs when the chocolate layer in pralines turns soft over time, or when the chocolate layer gets sensitive to touch.** Fat bloom can also occur on the chocolate layer, which happens mostly when different fats such as palm seed oil and cocoa butter are mixed.
Fat migration occurs when products with different fat systems come into contact with each other. The effect is most obvious when combining a hard fat (cocoa butter) and a soft fat or oil (praliné). The higher a product's fat content, the sooner migration will take place. Low fat products usually contain more solids, which prevents the development of the fat phase.

of fat bloom that generally occurs on dark chocolate, is created by the recrystallisation of the cocoa butter of the β form (beta) into it most stable form (VI form). In milk chocolate this is considerably slowed down by the presence of milk fat
- Incorrect storage conditions
- Touching with hands
- Fat migration. The fat in the centre (especially liquid oil) migrates to the chocolate shell. Depending on the fat content the chocolate shell will turn soft and the centre will harden over time.

Sugar bloom

Contrary to *fat bloom*, *sugar bloom* is a rough, irregular layer on top of the chocolate. *Sugar bloom* is always caused by condensation (moisture can settle on the chocolate that is removed from the refrigerator). This moisture will dissolve the sugar in the chocolate. When the water later evaporates, the sugar will be left behind in rough irregular crystals on the surface and give the chocolate an unattractive appearance. This phenomenon can occur after too cold a cooling, but mostly during warm, humid weather or too warm an environment.

Sugar bloom can be prevented by avoiding temperature fluctuations between cold and warm zones (and hence also condensation). Keep well packaged products, taken from a very cold area, long enough at room temperature before opening the packaging.

Sugar bloom is also created after machine enrobing, when the cooling tunnel is too cold, especially during warm, humid weather and/or too warm an environment.

This leads us to conclude that a respectable shelf life for a chocolate product is the result of an extensive series of processes:
- Formulating the centre
- The use of fresh and high quality ingredients
- The correct treatment of the ingredients
- Correct precrystallisation – of the centre as well! – when cocoa butter or chocolate is processed
- Hygienic conditions during processing
- Correct packaging materials
- Correct storage temperatures.

Fat bloom

Fat bloom is a phenomenon that is characterised by a grey film of fat crystals on the chocolate surface, which makes the chocolate lose its gloss.

Fat bloom is caused by recrystallisation of fats and/or the migration of a fat from the centre to the chocolate layer, which makes the chocolate softer and usually shows a lighter colour where the chocolate is in contact with the fat. In contrast to sugar bloom, the fat disappears when touched because it melts.

Fat bloom can be caused by:
- Incorrect or insufficient precrystallisation (see section on "Precrystallising")
- Recrystallisation of fats
- Excessive temperature difference between centre and chocolate during coating
- Incorrect cooling circumstances
- Recrystallisation. Even if the chocolate was processed correctly, *fat bloom* occurs over time. The type

Hygiene

In order to ensure maximum shelf life and avoid food contamination and/or poisoning, maximum attention should be paid to hygiene.

Food contamination and/or poisoning is caused by the presence of harmful or excessive quantities of micro-organisms. These micro-organisms develop quickly in the presence of foodstuffs, water, (usually) oxygen and at the right temperature and degree of acidity.

In the food industry it must be taken into account that food for humans is also food for micro-organisms. When food scraps are left behind on the floor or in appliances, micro-organisms can easily develop in them. Professionals have a huge responsibility towards their customers. When food contamination and/or poisoning is established, the results are catastrophic for the business manager.

Food poisoning: micro-organisms that produce toxic substances are present. In favourable conditions bacteria multiply by division every 20 to 30 minutes. In this example we start with one bacterium. Although micro-organisms are very small, they are able to multiply on a large scale, as they almost always appear in very large numbers (1,000,000 per gram of product).

Time	number of bacteria
0	1
20 min	2
40 min	4
1 hour	8
2 hours	64
3 hours	512
4 hours	4,096
5 hours	32,768
6 hours	262,144
7 hours	2,079,152
8 hours	16,777,216
9 hours	134,217,728
10 hours	1,073,741,824
Etc.	

It is impossible to prepare food without bacteria. Given this enormous potential for growth the aim is to limit the initial number of bacteria and to control the bacteria's growth conditions.

LIMITING THE NUMBER OF BACTERIA

- Be very discerning in terms of quality of basic ingredients.
- Ensure that equipment is constantly cleaned and regularly disinfected (use disinfectant in rinse water).
- Pay attention to your staff's personal hygiene methods.

CONTROLLING GROWTH CONDITIONS

- Temperature: the effect of temperature on growth is very significant.
- Most bacteria show the greatest growth between 10°C and 60°C (50-140°F).
- Bacteria growth is at its highest between 25-35°C (77-95°F).
- Foods are therefore somewhat safer above 60°C (140°F) and under 10°C (50°F).
- Foods can contain substances in which specific bacteria feel at home and in which they will multiply particularly fast. Water: without water micro-organisms cannot develop. This is why dry food has a long shelf life. However, dry products attract moisture from the air (sugar, milk powder, salt). This raises the moisture content in the product, which gives micro-organisms a chance of survival.
- Water activity: in order to check whether a product contains enough water to allow for the growth of micro-organisms, the water activity (Aw) must first be tested. More on this subject in the "Shelf life" section.

Factors that extend shelf life

As a result of the unavoidable physical and chemical changes in a recipe, which take place when mixing various ingredients, the product will become unsuitable for consumption in the long term and will be influenced by several external factors (sometimes organoleptic only).

The shelf life of pralines is always limited. Even with the most stringent hygiene and storage measures, most pralines prepared according to traditional methods cannot be kept for very long. 80% of the deterioration is caused by water. However, micro-organisms[1] also multiply in the presence of food (sugars, proteins, vitamins and salts) as well as heat.

WHAT CAN GO WRONG? /

PHYSICAL DETERIORATION
- Drying
- Moisture absorption
- Loss of aroma
- Sugar bloom
- Fat separation
- Fat bloom
- Undesirable crystallisation (through fats as well as sugars)
- Odour absorption

BACTERIOLOGICAL DETERIORATION
- Fungi
- Yeasts

CHEMICAL DETERIORATION
- Oxidation
- Saponification

WHAT ACTION TO TAKE? /

SHORT TERM SOLUTION
- Boiling: kills many micro-organisms; only spore formers remain active. Infection recurs after boiling.
- Pasteurising: 75-80°C (167-176°F) cuts the number of germs in micro-organisms.
- Sterilising: 130°C (266°F) kills all micro-organisms.

LONG TERM SOLUTION
- Reduce water activity as much as possible.
- Create a balance in relative humidity between the centre and its environment.
- Add alcohol to the recipe.
- Bring the pH value to 4.5.
- Candying: by adding sugar (or salt) water is extracted from the cell, which stops the development of micro organisms.
- Crystallising: applying a protective sugar layer around the centre.

- Cooling: chemical and enzymatic processes are slowed down. Micro-organisms multiply more slowly.
- Freezing: chemical and enzymatic processes are greatly slowed down.
- Drying: metabolism is stopped.
- Preservatives: these substances have an inhibiting effect on metabolism or cause the organism to die off.

REDUCE WATER ACTIVITY / **Water activity is expressed in Aw or ERH (Equilibrium Relative Humidity[2]).** The total moisture content of a recipe only provides limited information on its shelf life. Shelf life actually depends on the quantity of water available to micro-organisms and chemical reactions. (The water present can be available or bound to a lesser or greater degree.) The available water in centres is, after all, the culture medium for numerous micro-organisms such as fungi, yeasts and dangerous bacteria such as Salmonella and Listeria. The fact is that numerous ingredients – among which cream, milk, butter, fruit juice or fruit pulp – are mainly made up of water.

WHAT IS BOUND AND FREE WATER?
The ingredients used in a recipe all have a different capacity to bind with water until they are saturated. Excess water is water available for microbial deterioration.
The greater the water activity (quantity of free water) in a centre, the greater the odds the centre will contain micro-organisms after a few days or weeks, which can have very damaging results for consumers or which can affect the appearance of the praline (bursting open). Water activity is limited in the production of pralines that are completely safe for consumption for at least three weeks to one month. This is possible by dissolving water-soluble dry mass in the water or liquid. (See section on "Characteristics of the most frequently used ingredients").
Water activity can be measured with an appliance (a Aw meter). This device measures the relative humidity above the centre in a specific receptacle. This is why ERH (Equilibrium Relative Humidity) is referred to in some specialist literature.
A centre's water activity is measured around 18°C (65°F) and rendered in a scale from 0 to 1, whereby

~ 0 stands for complete dry mass or solids
~ 1 stands for 100% water
All gradations between 0 and 1 are therefore solutions, saturated to a greater or lesser degree by dissolving water-soluble components in them.

An Aw value of

< 0.61	the centre is safe from osmophilic yeasts
< 0.65	xerophilic fungi
< 0.75	halophilic bacteria (saline fungi)
< 0.80	regular fungi
< 0.85	staphylococci
< 0.88	regular yeasts
< 0.94	non-pathogenic bacteria[3]
< 0.95	pathogenic bacteria

These micro-organisms will not develop with lower Aw values than those indicated.

Aw	
> 0.85	can be kept up to three weeks
0.85 à > 0.6	can be kept up to three months
< 0.6	microbiologically stable

However: just similar to other products, products with a low Aw value can still contain traces of pathogenic micro-organisms. This means more specifically:

	the Aw in
chocolate and gianduja	< 0.30
Caramel	< 0.48
Marzipan	< 0.65-0.70
Fondant sugar	< 0.75-0.84
Butter creams	< 0.81-0.87 (average)
Ganaches	< 0.90-0.95 (average)

HOW CAN WATER ACTIVITY IN CENTRES BE REDUCED?
Centres for which the dissolved, fixed components content in water is higher than 87%, fall within a water activity of 0.6 or lower and therefore have quite a long shelf life.
Sugar combined with sugar substitutes and saturated sugar solutions such as glucose syrup, inverted sugar, dextrose, etc., are ideal for this purpose (depending on the respective solubility). Remember, however:
~ Water at 20°C (68°F) will dissolve twice its weight in sugar. Therefore, 50 g sugar is dissolved in 25 g water.
~ Be careful with ganaches: these are emulsions of water and fat (cream or butter), in which the fat does not dissolve in water! When mixing cream and chocolate a large mass of water or moisture remains subject to water activity.
~ Moisture content is indicated in percentages.

A product with a moisture content of 10% consists of 1/10 parts water.
A product with a moisture content of 50% consists of half water and half solids.
Remark: in some products reference is made to solid content. A solid content of 35% corresponds to a moisture content of 65%.

The water in a product is not 100% available to micro-organisms. One refers to "free water" and "bound water".

Moisture content = bound water + free water.

Micro-organisms require free water. Water activity determines the physical characteristics of a centre. In addition water activity also plays a significant role in the appearance and physical characteristics of a centre.
~ The more water a centre contains, the greater the odds that it will release moisture to its environment (if the centre's ERH is higher than that of the surrounding air). This causes drying, hardening, possible sugars can crystallise ... which affects the texture, taste and appearance of the pralines.
This process can be slowed down by letting the centre – for example of a cutting praline or truffle – "crust" overnight.
~ Praline centres with very low water activity can nonetheless absorb moisture from the environment. This can obviously also lead to the development of germs, bacteria, etc.

CREATE A BALANCE IN RELATIVE HUMIDITY BETWEEN THE CENTRE AND ITS ENVIRONMENT / This way the centre will neither absorb nor release moisture to its environment. By saturating the liquids in the centre, a balance in relative humidity is achieved. Such centres will at room temperature—and in constant

(European) climate conditions—neither absorb nor release moisture to the environment. In practice both aims are achieved by:
- replacing 50% of the sugar quantity with glucose syrup or glucose powder in liquid based centres;
- adding 10% sorbitol to the liquid quantity (cream) in ganaches;
- adding 50% glucose syrup to the liquid quantity in ganaches.

Even under optimum storage conditions pralines with a rather high water activity rate (fresh truffles based on cream, butter) cannot be kept for more than a few days, because of the risk of microbacteriological contamination. During production their only (but required!) protection consists in ensuring that the centre is completely enrobed by a sufficiently thick chocolate layer when dipping, that there are no holes, cracks, etc.
Packaging can also prevent moisture loss.
Monitor storage conditions and time: never take risks and remove the products from the shelf when in doubt!

ADD ALCOHOL TO THE RECIPE / **An easy way to make the centre microbiologically stable, is to add 17% alcohol at 94% of the total moisture content (water + alcohol) in the recipe.** This method is banned in most of the United States and in Muslim countries.

ADJUST ACIDITY DEGREE / **Bring the pH value to 4.5.** With a citric acid solution the pH value is adjusted until a pH of 4.2 to 4.7 is reached. Add 0.1% sorbic acid to the mixture. (Sorbic acid is a preservative).
Instead of sorbic acid, 0.1% (of the total) potassium sorbate can be added.
Warning! Check if this is allowed under the national Food and Drugs acts.

CANDYING / **Candying is one of the oldest preserving techniques, but one that is only applied to fruit, fruit rind and vegetables.** The technique consists of replacing the water in the fruit cells with highly concentrated sugar syrup, which will stop the development of microorganisms. This process must take place in steps and lasts about ten days. The concentration of the sugar syrup in which the fruit is placed, must be increased slowly, in order to achieve the interaction.

For operating method, see section on "Candying".

CRYSTALLISING / **Crystallising helps to protect the product against drying.** For operating method, see section on "Crystallising".

COOLING / **All manner of chemical and enzymatic processes take place in fresh ingredients and products.** In living products (fruit, grains) breathing reactions take place, whereby glucose reacts with oxygen and is broken down into carbon dioxide and water.
In addition to these changes reactions occur between the product itself and the oxygen in the air. This is how fat products can turn rancid. Vitamin loss can also take place or flavour, colour and taste can lose their quality. Briefly, the effect of cooling comes down to the fact that all these reactions are slowed down by lowering the temperature, so that the product keeps its fresh characteristics longer. The lower the temperature, the greater the delay. It is nonetheless impossible to fully stop these processes. Enzyme activity is still noticeable at -35°C (-31°F).

FREEZING / **When deep freezing chemical and enzymatic processes are slowed down more than when cooling.** A significant difference with cooling, is that when deep-freezing ice crystals are formed in the product. These ice crystals are made up of pure water. Consequences of the formation of ice crystals:
- The water that has turned into ice crystals, is extracted from the product. This has a drying effect. After thawing the product is sometimes unable to reabsorb all the moisture. In some centres this can result in curdling.
- The crystals can damage the product's cells.
- By freezing slowly these crystals become bigger. This causes the cell membranes to be pierced, the cells lose all their moisture and collapse when the product thaws. Result: the product turns stringy and dry.

Proper preliminary treatment can limit this deterioration in quality. It has been demonstrated that rapid freezing will considerably reduce the adverse consequences of crystal formation. Here it is primarily the speed with which the temperature range between 0°C (32°F) and -5°C (23°F) is bridged, because it is exactly in this temperature range that most crystals are formed.

Conclusion:
- When freezing slowly a rather small number of large crystals are created.
- When freezing rapidly a rather large number of small crystals are created.

In the latter case the water also remains better distributed in the product, so that after thawing it can be absorbed more rapidly and easily.

FREEZING PRALINES / **Flavour tests have demonstrated that the taste of deep frozen pralines is not affected providing they are properly packaged.** Furthermore, from the very beginning of the production process all products must display flawless flavour/quality. White chocolate that is already oxidised, will only continue to oxidise during the freezing process.

Ensure that there are no empty spaces in the "ballotins" (boxes), since the moisture present in the air can condense in them. This will result in the pralines in the top layer later showing sugar bloom. A lot of air also slows down the freezing process.

When thawing, the package should not be opened as long as the temperature of the content differs more than 10°C (18°F) from the ambient temperature. If this is not adhered to, condensation will be created on the products, which will later result in sugar bloom.

Liqueur pralines with a sugar crust cannot be frozen as they are prone to burst.

In pralines with fondant and alcohol inverting is slowed down. This will result in the centre not turning liquid as rapidly.

DRYING / **When moisture is extracted from the cells, micro-organisms no longer have food, which stops their metabolism.**

PRESERVATIVES / **See section on "Characteristics of the most frequently used ingredients".**

[1] Micro-organisms: single or multi cell groups. The main ones are: fungi, bacteria and yeasts. These are present everywhere; it is impossible to prevent infections when extracting, transporting and processing ingredients.

[2] Equilibrium Relative Humidity: ERH = the quantity of water (in %) present in the air at a specific temperature, compared to the maximum quantity of water that air can contain at that same temperature. (To be measured with a psychrometer or hygrometer.)

[3] Pathogenic: causes disease.

Sugar processing

Boiling sugar *58* / Sugar syrups *58* / Measuring equipment and conversions for sugar syrups *59* /
Brix - Baumé conversion at specific temperatures *60* / Recognising cooking points *62* /

Boiling sugar

When sugar is boiled, the sugar is dissolved and the mixture's water content is reduced to the desired quantity through evaporation.

The water content can be deducted from the boiling temperature: The higher the temperature, the less water. The correct relationship between cooking temperature and water content can be read in the table below.

Boiling point for sugar solutions

°C	°F	Water content in %
104	219.2	35.0
105	221.0	30.6
106	222.8	27.6
107	224.6	25.2
108	226.4	22.8
109	228.2	21.0
110	230.0	19.1
111	231.8	17.8
112	233.6	16.6
113	235.4	15.4
114	237.2	14.3
115	239.0	13.4
116	240.8	12.6
117	242.6	11.8
118	244.4	11.0
119	246.2	10.3
120	248.0	9.6
121	249.5	9.0
122	251.6	8.4
123	253.4	7.8
124	255.2	7.2
125	257.0	6.8
126	258.8	6.3
127	260.6	5.8
128	262.4	5.4
129	264.2	5.1
130	266.0	4.9

For items with a high water content (> 20%), the use of the boiling temperature as a means to determine the water content will not be precise enough. A refractometer yields a better result (especially when the mixture contains agar-agar or pectin).

In order to get even results some care is required when boiling sugar. The sugar must be fully dissolved before the cooking process starts. A simple method to achieve full solution, consists in mixing the sugar with 1/3 its weight in water and while stirring heating until all sugar crystals have disappeared. After the rims of the cooking vessel are brushed with water, the glucose is added and cooking continued.

In order to limit inverted sugar formation[1] to the greatest possible extent, rapid cooking is recommended. That is why you should use as strong a heat source as possible or work with small quantities. The cooking process should not last longer than 15 minutes.

Sugar syrups

WATER QUANTITY / A solution of sugar in water, boiled at a specific temperature, will always contain the same quantity of water at that temperature. If, for example, two syrups, one of which consists of 1,000 g sugar and 300 g water and the other of 1,000 g sugar and 600 g water, were to be heated to 110°C (230°F), then both syrups would contain the same water quantity, whenever they reached this boiling point.

SATURATED SUGAR SYRUPS / Whenever sugar is dissolved in water, and more sugar is added, the syrup will inevitably become saturated. No more sugar can be added as it will no longer dissolve.

Saturated sugar syrup contains a maximum of soluble sugar. Whenever the temperature is raised, more sugar can be added.

FOR EXAMPLE

100 g water is saturated at 15°C (59°F) by adding 196 g sugar (approx. 66% sugar)

20°C	(68°F)	203 g
30°C	(86°F)	221 g
50°C	(122°F)	260 g
60°C	(140°F)	286 g
100°C	(212°F)	487 g (approx. 83% sugar)

Water is mainly used to dissolve sugar crystals in sugar products. To this end at least 17% water is added to the sugar. If, however, the syrup is brought to the boil too quickly, a considerable quantity of water will evaporate and there will be too little water left to dissolve all the sugar. This is why it is recommended to use 23% water. Per 1,000 g sugar, add 300 g water (to ensure that the sugar crystals are dissolved when the syrup starts to boil).

This is why it is necessary to brush the edges of the bowl with water so as to remove all crystals.

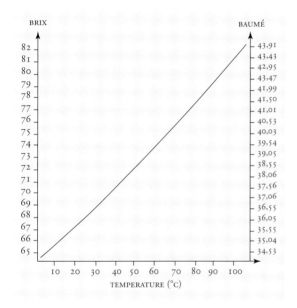

OVERSATURATED SUGAR SYRUPS / A warm saturated sugar solution that is cooled will contain an excess of sugar.

FOR EXAMPLE
- at 100°C (212°F) 100 g water will be saturated with 487 g sugar
- at 20°C (68°F) 100 g water will be saturated with 203 g sugar

When 100 g saturated water at 100°C (212°F) cools to 20°C (68°F) there is a sugar excess of 487 − 203 = 284 g. This excess will crystallise sooner or later.

For some applications it is advisable for the syrup to fully crystallise, as is the case for making fondant sugar and fudge. In this case crystallisation can be expedited by stirring the syrup, or by adding a little powdered

sugar for seeding. For other applications it is advisable for the syrup to partially crystallise, as is the case for making liqueur chocolates and candied syrup.

Whenever sugar syrup is heated above 104°C (220°F), and subsequently cooled to ambient temperature, an oversaturated sugar solution is created, and there is a risk of crystallisation.

This represents a problem in the case of caramels and hard sugar products. This is why glucose is added to such products to slow down crystallisation.

Measuring apparatus and conversions for sugar syrups

BAUMÉMETER (DENSITY METER OR SUGAR SCALE) / When sugar syrups are heated, water evaporates. This results in the syrup's specific gravity increasing and the Baumémeter not sinking as deeply into the syrup. The indication of the scale varies from 0°B in 17°C (62.6°F) water to 50°B.[2] Syrup density is temperature dependent.

FOR EXAMPLE
warm sugar syrup of 33°B will indicate 36°B in cold conditions and weigh 1,360 g. The water content for a sugar syrup is approximately 60% for a 20°B-syrup.

27°B	50.0 %
30°B	45.0 %
33°B	40.0 %
36°B	32.0 %
40°B	25.0 %
43°B	14.0 %
45°B	9.0 %
48°B	6.5 %

To obtain a correct scale indication the Baumémeter must be rinsed and dried after each weighing, otherwise the meter will sink deeper because of the sticky sugar. The accuracy of the measurement is also determined by syrup temperature.

Baumé degrees were once used frequently, but are increasingly replaced by the Brix scale, which is more accurate.

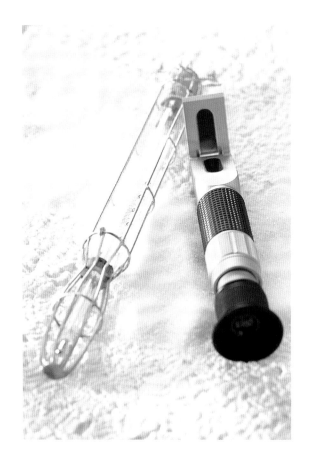

Refractometer / The refractometer is an optical instrument that provides a simple, fast and accurate measurement of dry components of sugar-containing syrups such as jellies, fruit syrups and some fillings.

The refractometer determines the light refraction index[3] of solids (or liquids). Because of its user-friendliness the meter is often used in the sugar, milk and pharmaceutical industries. The measurement unit is degrees Brix. A small version, the pocket refractometer, is very handy for chocolatiers.

Note: there are refractometers for thin syrups from 0 to 50° Brix, for thick syrups from 45 to 82° Brix and for all syrups from 0 to 90° Brix.

Brix - Baumé conversion at specific temperatures

The table below shows that the accuracy of both measuring techniques depends on the temperature at which the measurement is taken.

Brix		Baumé		Celsius	
15°C	boiling at	15°C	boiling at	grams	
10	1.5	5.5	1.4	100	100.4
20	12.9	11.3	7.5	200	100.6
30	23.1	16.8	13.1	300	101.0
40	33.3	22.3	18.9	400	101.5
45	38.5	25.0	21.6	450	101.7
47	40.5	26.1	22.7	470	101.8
50	43.5	27.7	24.3	500	102.0
52	45.6	28.8	25.4	520	102.2
54	47.6	29.8	26.4	540	102.4
56	49.6	30.9	27.5	560	102.6
58	51.7	31.9	28.5	580	102.8
60	53.7	33.0	29.6	600	103.0
62	55.7	34.0	30.6	620	103.5
64	57.8	36.1	31.7	640	103.9
66	59.8	36.1	32.7	660	104.6
68	61.8	37.1	33.7	680	105.5
70	63.9	38.1	34.7	700	106.5
72	65.9	39.1	35.7	720	107.1
74	67.9	40.1	36.7	740	107.8
76	69.9	41.1	37.7	760	109.0
78	72.0	42.1	38.7	780	111.0
80	74.0	43.1	39.7	800	113.0

Brix	Baumé	Brix	Baumé	Brix	Baumé	Brix	Baumé
1.0	0.56	25.5	14.11	50.0	27.28	74.5	39.79
1.5	0.84	26.0	14.39	50.5	27.54	75.0	40.03
2.0	1.12	26.5	14.66	51.0	27.81	75.5	40.28
2.5	1.40	27.0	14.93	51.5	28.07	76.0	40.53
3.0	1.68	27.5	15.20	52.0	28.33	76.5	40.77
3.5	1.96	28.0	15.48	52.5	28.59	77.0	41.01
4.0	2.24	28.5	15.75	53.0	28.86	77.5	41.26
4.5	2.52	29.0	16.02	53.5	29.12	78.0	41.50
5.0	2.79	29.5	16.29	54.0	29.38	78.5	41.74
5.5	3.07	30.0	16.57	54.5	29.64	79.0	41.99
6.0	3.35	30.5	16.84	55.0	29.90	79.5	42.23
6.5	3.63	31.0	17.11	55.5	30.16	80.0	42.47
7.0	3.91	31.5	17.38	56.0	30.42	80.5	42.71
7.5	4.19	32.0	17.65	56.5	30.68	81.0	42.95
8.0	4.46	32.5	17.92	57.0	30.94	81.5	43.19
8.5	4.74	33.0	18.19	57.5	31.20	82.0	43.43
9.0	5.02	33.5	18.46	58.0	31.46	82.5	43.67
9.5	5.30	34.0	18.73	58.5	31.71	83.0	43.91
10.0	5.57	34.5	19.00	59.0	31.97	83.5	44.15
10.5	5.85	35.0	19.28	59.5	32.23	84.0	44.38
11.0	6.13	35.5	19.55	60.0	32.49	84.5	44.62
11.5	6.41	36.0	19.81	60.5	32.74	85.0	44.86
12.0	6.68	36.5	20.08	61.0	33.00	85.5	45.09
12.5	6.96	37.0	20.35	61.5	33.26	86.0	45.33
13.0	7.24	37.5	20.62	62.0	33.51	86.5	45.57
13.5	7.51	38.0	20.89	62.5	33.77	87.0	45.80
14.0	7.79	38.5	21.16	63.0	34.02	87.5	46.03
14.5	8.07	39.0	21.43	63.5	34.28	88.0	46.27
15.0	8.34	39.5	21.70	64.0	34.53	88.5	46.50
15.5	8.62	40.0	21.97	64.5	34.79	89.0	46.73
16.0	8.89	40.5	22.23	65.0	35.04	89.5	46.96
16.5	9.17	41.0	22.50	65.5	35.29	90.0	47.20
17.0	9.45	41.5	22.77	66.0	35.55	90.5	47.43
17.5	9.72	42.0	23.04	66.5	35.80	91.0	47.66
18.0	10.00	42.5	23.30	67.0	36.05	91.5	47.89
18.5	10.27	43.0	23.57	67.5	36.30	92.0	48.12
19.0	10.55	43.5	23.84	68.0	36.55	92.5	48.35
19.5	10.82	44.0	24.10	68.5	36.81	93.0	48.58
20.0	11.10	44.5	24.37	69.0	37.06	93.5	48.80
20.5	11.37	45.0	24.63	69.5	37.31	94.0	49.03
21.0	11.65	45.5	24.90	70.0	37.56	94.5	49.26
21.5	11.92	46.0	25.17	70.5	37.81	95.0	49.49
22.0	12.20	46.5	25.43	71.0	38.06	95.5	49.72
22.5	12.47	47.0	25.70	71.5	38.30	96.0	49.94
23.0	12.74	47.5	25.96	72.0	38.55	96.5	50.16
23.5	13.02	48.0	26.23	72.5	38.80	97.0	50.39
24.0	13.29	48.5	26.49	73.0	39.05	97.5	50.61
24.5	13.57	49.0	26.75	73.5	39.30	98.0	50.84
25.0	13.84	49.5	27.02	74.0	39.54	98.5	51.06
						99.0	51.28
						99.5	51.51
						100.0	51.73

Recognising cooking points

If you do not own a Baumé and refractometer, you can still get along by "feeling" the syrup consistency. Before the aforementioned meters existed, this feeling method was applied. It does nonetheless require some experience. The various cooking points give the syrup a name that somewhat clarifies its consistency.

Pure sugar solutions in water at high temperatures clearly have a different image from sugar syrups containing 20% glucose.

Simple syrups	Syrups containing 20% glucose	Name
104°C (219°F)	106°C (223°F)	Pearl
106°C (223°F)	108°C (226°F)	Thread
108°C (226°F)	110°C (230°F)	Soft blow
110°C (230°F)	111°C (232°F)	Hard blow
113°C (235°F)	114°C (239°F)	Soft ball
114°C (237°F)	117°C (242°F)	Firm ball
117°C (242°F)	120°C (248°F)	Hard ball
122°C (252°F)	125°C (257°F)	Soft crack
127°C (260°F)	141°C (286°F)	Pulled sugar
135°C (275°F)	145-150°C (239-302°F)	Hard crack

HOW CAN VARIOUS COOKING POINTS BE RECOGNISED?

- Pearl: If the syrup rolls from the skimmer in pearls (32° Baumé).
- Grain: Sugar forms a thin thread between the fingers (35-36° Baumé).
- Small blow: Take the skimmer from the syrup; when blowing on it small balls will appear (37-38° Baumé).
- Large blow: Same as above, with bigger and firmer balls (38-39° Baumé).
- Soft ball: Remove a small quantity of syrup with a spatula, drop it into water at room temperature. A small soft ball is formed.
- Firm ball: Same as above, with slightly firmer ball.
- Hard ball: Firmer still.
- Soft crack: Remove the flattened sample from the water. Is should bend before breaking.

- Pulled sugar: Same as above, but firmer. The sugar still sticks to the teeth.
- Hard crack: The sample breaks immediately and no longer sticks to the teeth.
- Caramel: The sugar turns a golden brown.

[1] During the cooking process a percentage of the sugar is always converted into inverted sugar. Inverted sugar has an adverse effect on all hard, non-crystallised products (hygroscopicity increases). In crystallised products an excess of inverted sugar can nonetheless considerably slow down further crystallisation.

[2] See section on "Sugar syrups".

[3] The light changes direction as it moves from one environment to the next. The angle between the incoming light and the outgoing light is the breaking index.

Celsius	Fahrenheit	Celsius	Fahrenheit	Celsius	Fahrenheit
-12.2	10	25	77	79.4	175
-10	14	26	78.8	80	176
-9.5	15	26.6	80	82.2	180
-6.6	20	27	80.6	85	185
-5	23	28	82.4	87.7	190
-3.8	25	29	84.2	90	194
-1.1	30	29.4	85	90.5	195
0	32	30	86	93.3	200
1	33.8	31	87.8	95	203
1.6	35	32	89.6	96.1	205
2	35.6	32.2	90	98.8	210
3	37.4	33	91.4	100	212
4	39.2	34	93.2	101.7	215
4.4	40	35	95	104.4	220
5	41	36	96.8	105	221
6	42.8	37	98.6	107.2	225
7	44.6	37.7	100	110	230
7.2	45	38	100.4	112.8	235
8	46.4	39	102.2	115	239
9	48.2	40	104	115.6	240
10	50	40.5	105	118.4	245
11	51.8	43.3	110	120	248
12	53.6	45	113	121.1	250
12.7	55	46.1	115	123.9	255
13	55.4	48.8	120	125	257
14	57.2	50	122	126.7	260
15	59	51.6	125	129.5	265
15.5	60	54.4	130	130	266
16	60.8	55	131	132.2	270
17	62.6	57.2	135	135	275
18	64.4	60	140	137.8	280
18.3	65	62.7	145	140	284
19	66.2	65	149	140.6	285
20	68	65.5	150	143.4	290
21	69.8	68.3	155	145	293
21.1	70	70	158	146.1	295
22	71.6	71.1	160	148.9	300
23	73.4	73.8	165	150	302
23.8	75	75	167	151.7	305
24	75.2	76.6	170	154.5	310

$$^{\circ}F - 32 \times 5/9 = {}^{\circ}C \qquad {}^{\circ}C \times 9/5 + 32 = {}^{\circ}F$$

06

Starting out

Starting tools *66* / More advanced equipment *68* / Crystallising *69* /
Candying fruits and vegetables *70* / Liqueur chocolates *72* / Caramel syrups and creams *75* /
Different flavours in caramel creams *76* / Fondant sugar dough *77* / Fudge *78* / Sugar panning *81* /

Starting tools

Sugar and chocolate processing is a speciality that requires specific basic working tools, such as pallet knives, triangular and cutting knives, a rolling pin, spatulas and spoons.

TWO CUTTING ROLLS WITH EXCHANGEABLE KNIVES /
To portion out and cut or, if no wire slicer is available, to score the surface of praline centres that will later be cut with a knife.

DIPPING FORKS /
With two, three or four prongs and one round to dip centres and to apply decorations on the surface of the chocolates.

BOWLS (PLASTIC AND STAINLESS STEEL) /
preferably no copper bowls (these are outdated and represent a risk of flavour impairment and verdigris poisoning).

STAINLESS STEEL POTS /
are suitable for various heat sources.

NON-STICK MATS, SILPAT AND FLEXIPAN MOULDS FOR FRUIT DOUGH /
Manufacturer: see www.demarle.com

AN EXTENSIVE SUPPLY OF FLAT METAL OR PLASTIC SHEETS AND PLATES WITH UPRIGHT EDGES /
Sizes depend on working comfort, dimensions of cooling space and racks.

COOLING SPACE WITH INTERNAL VENTILATION /

STAINLESS STEEL COUNTERTOPS /
Covered in marble or another mineral, the top can also be man-made. Under no circumstances should you use wood! (Due to bacterial contamination: yeasts, fungi and bacteria settle in the wood's minuscule pores.)

A SUFFICIENT NUMBER OF RACKS AND STORAGE SPACE /

CHOCOLATE MELTING PANS / with various options:

DOUBLE-SIDED OIL BATH: OUTDATED
disadvantages:
- does not react fast enough to temperature changes
- very slow cooling
- heavy and cumbersome
- very expensive
- high energy consumption
- difficult to clean
advantages:
- none

DOUBLE-SIDED WATER BATH: OUTDATED
disadvantages:
- does not react fast enough to temperature changes
- slow cooling
- heavy and cumbersome
- very expensive
- risk of water and vapour contamination
- some systems require water connection
- difficult to keep chocolate crystallisation process under control
- difficult to clean
- high energy consumption
advantages:
- none

HOT AIR THROUGH HEATING ELEMENTS THAT KEEP THE SPACE UNDER THE CHOCOLATE BOWL WARM
disadvantages:
- difficult to clean
- high energy consumption
advantages
- keeps chocolate crystallisation process pretty well under control

CONDUCTION SYSTEM
the double sides provide contact heat by heat transfer to the chocolate tray.

disadvantages:
- none
advantages:
- chocolate crystallisation process can be easily kept under control all day
- it is even possible to start work after melting without

pre-crystallisation, if the chocolate chunks melt very slowly overnight so that a thick but soft layer remains on the surface the next morning. For the soft layer was overcrystallised. By thoroughly mixing this layer with the warm bottom layer, the chocolate is pre-crystallised. If necessary heat a little.

- ~ low energy consumption
- ~ easy maintenance
- ~ cheap
- ~ comes in several sizes: small round (3.5 kg size) suitable for dipping fork and decorations. 7.5 kg, 10-12 kg and 20 kg sizes

Manufacturer: see www.moldart.be

SUFFICIENT NUMBER OF CHOCOLATE MOULDS /

the best ones are made of polycarbonate (Macrolon)
Manufacturers: see www.jkvnl.com, www.chocolate-world.be, www.moldart.be

CANDYING PANS /

cone-shaped metal trays with a grid at the bottom to prevent items to be candied from lying on the bottom. A second grid prevents items from floating.

SUGAR THERMOMETER /

glass tube, protected by a metal cage, with graduations of 40-220°C (104-428°F), to measure the cooking degree of sugar syrups.

BAUMÉ METER OR SUGAR SCALE /

glass tube with graduations of 0 to 45° Baumé. Weights are attached to the bottom so that the meter floats on the density of sugar syrups. A matching narrow elongated beaker is ¾ filled with sugar syrup. The meter floats in the syrup. The graduation on the syrup surface indicates the Baumé degree. In theory the syrup should be measured at room temperature, but in practice it is much easier and faster to measure the boiled syrup; in this case the difference must be taken into consideration (see sections on "Measuring devices and conversions" and "Brix-Baumé Conversion").

SCALE /
preferably digital with tare option.

MIXER /

More advanced equipment

REFRACTOMETER /
optical instrument that indicates the percentage of sugars in a syrup by means of the light refraction index (see section on "Measuring devices and conversions").

PRALINE CUTTING APPARATUS / **ideal for cutting all manner of flat material quickly and neatly.** Suitable for cutting ganaches, butter creams, marzipan and jellies. Comes standard with a base, a scooping plate and five different cutting frames, allowing for various combinations and sizes. Frame sizes: 7.5 mm, 15 mm, 22.5 mm, 30 mm en 37.5 mm.
Manufacturer: see www.dedy.de

MOULDING APPLIANCE / **multifunctional appliance to melt, cool and precystallise chocolate.** Funnel facilitates centre of the moulds. The chocolate is aired on the vibration table, and the excess chocolate runs back from the mould into the appliance's supply chamber through the dripping rack. Ideal for long-term use, as the chocolate retains the correct quantity of crystals all day long. Whenever there is the least tendency to thicken, all that is required is to raise the temperature by 0.5 to 1°, so as to maintain the correct balance between crystal growth and melting of excess of added crystals. Manufacturer: see www.moldart.be

FOOD PROCESSOR /
powerful cutter to create various doughs and creams, refining nuts, fast melting and pre-crystallising of very small quantities of chocolate.

ENROBER / **an appliance with a conveyor belt on which centres are placed.** They are carried under a chocolate curtain and are fully coated with a thin layer of chocolate. Excess chocolate can be vibrated or blown

off to achieve the desired shell thickness. The pralines are then transferred to a paper belt, or in more expensive versions a cooling tunnel from which they emerge ready for use and immediate packaging.
Manufacturer: see www.dedy.de

Crystallising

Crystallising is enrobing sugar and chocolate items with a thin coat of sugar.
In order to:
~ Make soft products stronger
~ Prevent drying
~ Give an attractive appearance
~ Extend shelf life

Heat 1,000 gr sugar and 350 gr water to 32-33° Baumé (60-62° Brix); this is about 105°C (221°F).

As soon as the syrup starts to boil, brush the edges of the bowl with water. There should be no dissolved crystals left.
At this point do not stir the syrup!
Heat the syrup until the boiling temperature is reached and then it let cool.
As soon as the syrup is no longer too hot, cover it with plastic film (the film must be in contact with the syrup).
Let the syrup reach room temperature in an area that is free from movement or vibration.
Arrange the products in a high sided pan. Do not place the products against each other; this will guarantee a good result.
Preferably crystallise at the end of a working day, to prevent vibrations or tremors that would affect the crystallising pan.
Carefully pour the syrup on the products, until they are fully covered.
Place a grid on the syrup; this will stop the products from rising to the surface. (Crystallising pans with matching grid are available on the market.)

After about 24 hours carefully turn over the pan with the grid, to drain the syrup. Remove the pan and let the separated products dry on the grid.

The crystallising syrup can be reused several times. To reuse, add a little water and bring the syrup back to the right degree .
Warning: The recipe in the footnote cannot be reused without measuring device.

Candying fruits and vegetables

Candying is saturating fruits and vegetables with sugar, to prevent decay.
The cell content of fruits and vegetables is mostly made up of moisture in which substances such as sugars, acids, starch, proteins, etc., are present. The moisture percentage is high (on average 85%), which turns the dissolved substances and the moisture into an ideal culture medium for bacteria.
To preserve the fruits moisture is extracted from the cells by means of osmosis and replaced with sugar syrup. The fruits will then contain too little moisture for the bacteria.
If the fruits are correctly candied, and properly packaged against further drying, they can be kept for at least one year without cooling.
Good preparation of the fruits is required. Use only attractive and firm fruits, preferably before they are fully ripe. Avoid damaged or overripe fruits.

Most fruits and some vegetables can be used for this purpose.
Most common: Apricots, Pineapple, Angelica[3], Cherries, Lemons (slices or rind only), Oranges (whole, in parts, slices or rind only), Chestnuts, Plums, Bananas.
Less common, but tasty: Green almonds, Green nuts, Watermelons, Strawberries, Figs, Some vegetables.

The fruits must first be blanched or bleached. Effective blanching is important for a successful end result. Insufficient blanching will later result in the fruits shrinking; excessive blanching will turn the fruits into a pulp. Dip the fruits into hot, but not boiling, salted water. Remove the fruits with the help of a skimmer, as they come to the surface, and immediately place them in cold water, which should be changed a few times. Blanching changes the cell wall structure: this results in the fruit being able to absorb sugar more easily.
During actual candying the fruits are placed in a sugar syrup, which must contain a gradually higher sugar concentration every day, so that the sugar can permeate slowly through the cell pores.

The full process takes about two weeks.
- *1st day:* boil sugar syrup of 1 kg sugar and 600 g water to 20° Baumé (36° Brix). Place the drained fruits im-

mediately in the hot sugar syrup and allow to rest for 24 hours. A grid over the fruits prevents them from floating.

~ *2nd day:* drain the fruits (use the grid). Add 100 g sugar to the remaining syrup and heat to 22° Baumé (40° Brix). Pour the syrup over the fruits and let rest another 24 hours.

~ *3rd day:* drain the fruits again and add 100 g sugar to the syrup. Heat the syrup to 24° Baumé (44° Brix), pour over the fruits and allow to rest 24 hours.

~ *4th day:* see 3rd day (drain, heat syrup to 24° Baumé (44° Brix), add 100 g sugar.

~ *5th day:* see above, but heat to 26° Baumé (47° Brix).

~ *6th day:* see 5th day.

~ *7th day:* see above, but heat to 28° Baumé (51° Brix).

~ *8th day:* see 7th day.

~ *9th day:* see above, but heat to 30° Baumé (54° Brix).

~ *10th day:* see 9th day.

~ *11th day:* see above, but heat to 32° Baumé (58° Brix).

~ *12th day:* see above, but add 20 g glucose and heat the syrup to 34° Baumé (62° Brix).

~ The fruits will marinate for four days in this syrup.

Drain the fruits and package them carefully. Preferably keep them in a cooler (not a requirement).

~ Some fruits – such as chestnuts – will, in addition, be slightly iced to make them more attractive.

~ Thoroughly drain the candied fruits.

~ Prepare a sugar syrup with 1,000 g sugar and 300 g water, and bring the syrup to a boil, to 115°C (239°F). Dip the candied fruit into the syrup for a few minutes. Carefully rub the syrup against the edge of the bowl with a spatula, until slight crystallisation occurs. Gradually mix the white deposit with the fruit, until it is fully coated.

Warning! Only slight crystallisation should occur otherwise the dried end product will show dull white spots!

Liqueur chocolates

With sugar crust or without... both have advantages and disadvantages.

WITHOUT SUGAR CRUST / **Alcohol erodes chocolate.** Since there is no protective layer between the chocolate and the alcohol, the chocolate starts to turn soft after three to four weeks; the aroma changes, the chocolate loses its gloss and the pralines slowly start to collapse.

The higher the alcohol content, the faster the ensuing breakdown.

For this reason and also because liqueur is too liquid, too expensive, and sometimes tastes too strong when combined with chocolate, the liqueur is usually slightly thickened with sugar syrup. The sugar syrup can also help to crystallise any cracks resulting from any potential minuscule leaks.

Warning: liqueur syrups must be correctly saturated[5] on full cooling , if not they may crystallise over time.

There are several recipes.

1,000 g sugar, 500 g water, 1,000 g liqueur concentrate 54°
- Bring the sugar and water to the boil.
- Brush the edges of the bowl with water, as soon as the boiling point is reached.
- Continue to heat the syrup to 104°C (220°F).
- Then let the syrup cool to under 80°C (176°F) (preferably lukewarm).
- Pour the syrup on 1,000 g liqueur concentrate at 54° and mix without stirring.
- This yields a sugar syrup of approximately 23%.

Tip: it is easier to divide the liqueur between two bottles first and pour the lukewarm syrup into them. Seal the bottles immediately in order to prevent alcohol evaporation. Mix liqueur and syrup by shaking vigorously.

1,000 g sugar, 1,000 g water, 1,000 g glucose
- Bring the sugar and water to the boil.
- Brush the edges of the bowl with water, and continue to heat to 104°C (220°F).
- Leave the syrup until lukewarm.
- Per 500 g syrup 200 to 300 g liqueur concentrate is added.
- Cover immediately and shake vigorously.
- 200 g liqueur yields a 15% liqueur syrup
- 300 g liqueur yields a 20% liqueur syrup

2,600 g sugar, 1,000 g water, 800 g glucose
- Bring the sugar and water to the boil.
- Brush the edges of the bowl with water, and continue to heat to 106°C (222°F).
- Leave the syrup until lukewarm.
- 1,000 g of this syrup is mixed with
    360 g liqueur at 40°
    or 300 g liqueur at 50°
    or 240 g liqueur at 60°
- For a somewhat less liquid syrup, 0.2% gum Arabic or 0.5% agar/agar is added to these recipes.

Tip: a new method is based on thickening an alcohol-based sugar syrup with pectin, as the latter is more easily processed in the chocolate shell. Just before the syrup is poured into the bowl, an enzyme is mixed in. This specific enzyme breaks down the thickening action of the pectin.

WITH SUGAR CRUST / Is afterwards dipped in chocolate.

PRINCIPLE
As a result of moisture loss, but also through cooling, the sugar syrup becomes oversaturated. To correct this, part of the sugar crystallises. The liqueur syrup must have a sugar concentration of 34° Baumé or 65° Brix.

If the concentration is
- too high → crust too thick or full crystallisation
- too low → thin or no crust.

1,000 g sugar, 400 g water, 150 g liqueur, 50 g alcohol
- Bring the sugar and water to the boil.
- Brush the edges of the bowl with water, and continue to heat for a short time.
- Pour half the syrup in another bowl, and cool as quickly as possible to less than 80°C (176°F), while the other half continues to heat to 111°C (232°F).
- Mix the liqueur with the lukewarm syrup by pouring the mixture into another bowl a few times. The mixture must not be stirred!
- Add the hot syrup in the same way, by transferring to another bowl a few times.
- Carefully cover the liqueur syrup and leave to cool to less than 40°C (104°F).
- Meanwhile, dry starch at approximately 40°C (104°F) is sifted in a high sided pan, and levelled with a straight slat. Imprints are made in the starch surface with plaster moulds glued to a slat.
- Pour the liqueur into the imprints
- After approximately 30 minutes sift a little starch over them.
- Place in a heat chamber at a temperature no higher than 45°C (113°F), to avoid the formation of blisters on the liqueur centres.

- Approximately four hours later turn over the centres in the starch.
- Allow to stand overnight.
- The following morning remove the centres from the starch, place them in a sieve and remove powder carefully with a soft brush.
- After cooling they are dipped in dark chocolate.

Warning: Starch suitable for liqueur pralines, has to spend at least 20 to 30 hours in a heat chamber at approximately 100°C (212°F).

The starch must be dry, otherwise thick lumps of dried starch and sugar will stick to the liqueur centres.

WITH SUGAR CRUST IN MOULDED PRALINES / This is the fastest and simplest method. The chocolate shell is protected against the alcohol by a thin sugar crust.

PRINCIPLE

The chocolate shells are poured and, after hardening, are filled with a slightly oversaturated liqueur syrup. Overnight a slight crust appears on the edges and on the surface. The mould can then be closed with liquid chocolate.

1,500 g sugar, 500 g water, 50 g glucose,
150 g liqueur concentrate 60°, 150 g alcohol
- Bring the sugar and water to the boil.
- Carefully brush the edges of the bowl with water. Add glucose.
- Continue to heat the syrup to 106/107°C (223 to 225°F).
- Afterwards leave to cool to approximately 50°C (122°F) before mixing the liqueur and the alcohol by transferring between two bowls.

It is important in all recipes to strictly adhere to the boiling point.
- Undercooked → no crystal formation
- Overcooked → sugar crust too thick

The higher the degree of alcohol, the coarser the crystal formation. Sugar is not soluble in alcohol.

In order to avoid undesirable crystal formation, the syrup should never be stirred, when the syrup's temperature exceeds 102°C (215°F).

Warning: in order to avoid undesirable premature crystallisation unsaturated syrups should never be stirred.

Caramel syrups and creams

There are two methods of caramelising: either with or without liquid.

WITHOUT LIQUID / Sugar, glucose or sugar combined with glucose is heated under constant stirring until the mixture changes colour. Depending on the desired flavour, the mixture should be heated until the expected colour is achieved. Medium brown provides a pleasant caramel flavour, dark brown tastes bitter.

In order to prevent the syrup from turning too dark during the melting process of the sugar crystals, several options are available.

Melting all of the sugar at the same time causes lumps that are difficult to liquefy. In the meantime the melted portion continues to caramelise and the syrup turns too dark. This can be prevented by adding a small quantity (approximately 5%) of glucose or butter, or a few drops of lemon juice.

Another solution is melting a small quantity of sugar and only when that is melted, add a little more sugar, until all sugar is processed.

WITH LIQUID / Bring 1,000 gr sugar and 300 gr water to a boil.

Above the boiling point the edges of the bowl are brushed with water in order to melt out the last remaining crystals. Otherwise there is a risk that by further heating the sugar could suddenly fully crystallise into a sugar lump.

At around 145°C (239°F) the water is fully evaporated and the colouring process will start slowly.

Since part of the sucrose is converted into invert sugar during the heating process, and the change in colour also occurs, there is no further risk of crystallisation.

RECIPES /

CARAMEL SAUCE (WITH LONG SHELF LIFE OF AT LEAST ONE YEAR)

Suitable for making fondant sugar softer and for flavouring creams. Ideal for ice cream dishes.

	Recipe	Sugar and glucose-melting time in minutes	Total cooking time	Remarks	Aw-value
1.	500 g sugar 500 g cream 125 g butter	8	9. 50	Upon induction the sugar crystallises on the edges of the bowl. Colour: dark brown.	0.842
2.	500 g sugar 150 g water 500 g cream 125 g butter	13. 21	14. 30	Upon induction the edges stay clean. Colour: somewhat lighter than recipe 1.	0.796
3.	400 g sugar 100 g glucose 500 g cream 125 g butter	7. 10	9. 05	Sugar with glucose. Sugar does not get lumpy. Colour: warm light brown.	0.828
4.	250 g sugar 250 g glucose 500 g cream 125 g butter	8. 43	10. 50	Colour: see recipe 3.	0.844
5.	500 g glucose 500 g cream 125 g butter	11	14. 11	Colour: see recipes 3 and 4.	0.860

3,000 g sugar, 1,300 g water, 1,000 g glucose
- ~ Caramelise the sugar until it becomes a medium-brown colour. Quench very carefully with small quantities of warm water.
- ~ Add glucose and bring back to a boil.
- ~ Leave to cool and pour into bottles. Seal bottles.

CARAMEL CREAM FOR MOULDED CHOCOLATES
400 g sugar, 100 g glucose, 500 g cream, 200 g butter, 250 g milk chocolate, 75 g cognac

BASIC CARAMEL CREAM FOR MOULDINGS
Of: 1,000 g sugar, 1,000 g cream, 250 g butter (Aw: 0,782)
Of: 1,000 g glucose, 1,000 g cream, 250 g butter (Aw: 0.800)
Of: 1,000 g sugar, 300 g water, 1,000 g cream, 250 g boter (Aw: 0.796)
- ~ Caramelise the sugar as described earlier.
- ~ Slowly and carefully quench with the cream.
- ~ Continue to heat to ensure that all sugar is melted.
- ~ If desired add ginger at the end of the heating process. [6]

- ~ Leave the mixture to cool slowly and only then add the butter. When the butter is added to the boiling caramel, much of the butter flavour is lost. When margarine or another fat is used instead of butter, it also will get heated quickly, in order to neutralise the fatty flavour.

For further finishing touches, see "Caramel bowls" and "Marquise".

Different flavours in caramel creams

Comparative tests and results whereby on the one hand the sugar is caramelised dry or first dissolved in water and on the other hand the glucose/sugar ratio has increased from 0% to 100%.

EVALUATION
1. Soft creamy texture. Strong caramel flavour.

2. Caramel flavour quickly disappears from mouth.
3. Faint caramel flavour.
4. Faint caramel flavour.
5. Good flavour.

Remarks: These tests were carried out on induction hobs. Other heat sources heat more slowly and can favourably influence the caramel flavour with the Maillard reaction.

The Aw indication was only provided to give an overall idea. Obviously the Aw value is dependent on cooking time and the latter is subject to strong fluctuations.

Fondant sugar dough

Fondant is a white, sweet creamy dough. The dough is made up of minuscule sugar crystals in a saturated sugar solution. The fineness of the sugar crystals is a determining factor in its creaminess. Under no circumstances should the sugar crystals be tasted (on the palate). Fondant is used quite frequently in chocolate making around the world.

Mixed in centres it determines sweetness. As a bulking agent fondant increases volume and lowers cost price.

- The ERH for fondant sugar dough is approximately 75-80%.
- The ERH for cream fondant is approximately 80-85%.

It is one of the basic ingredients and is generally not made from scratch, but bought.

It is still useful to know the preparation method and to understand its principle, in order to be able to come up with new creations.

Water can be replaced with cream, condensed milk, soy or coconut milk. Fruit purees can be added, sugar can be replaced with maple syrup, etc. Adding frappé increases airiness and gives the fondant sugar dough an attractive white colour. To obtain very white fondant a minimum quantity of blue colouring is added.

In order to make the fondant slightly less sweet 2-3% fat is added. (This also increases the creamy appearance that is appreciated by the palate).

RECIPES /

STANDARD RECIPE (SEMI SOLID)
1,000 g sugar, 300 g water, 100 g glucose, 117°C (243°F)

STANDARD RECIPE (CREAM FONDANT)
1,000 g sugar, 300 g water, 200 g glucose, 115°C (239°F)

STANDARD RECIPE (CREAM FONDANT WITH TARTAR INSTEAD OF GLUCOSE)
1,000 g sugar, 300 g water, 12 g cream of tartar, 120°C (248°F)

~ Bring sugar and water to the boil.
~ Brush the edges of the pan to melt any remaining crystals. These crystals can crystallise the syrup prematurely and create a course texture.
~ Add the glucose (or cream of tartar) and continue to heat until the recommended temperature is reached.
~ Cool the syrup to approximately 30°C (86°F) before kneading it.
~ If the syrup is too hot, is crystallises too rapidly resulting in coarse crystal structure. If the crystal is too cold, it will crystallise slowly and with great difficulty.

Kneading can be done in two ways:
~ The warm syrup is poured onto a marble slab. Once the syrup is lukewarm, it is worked with two triangular knives. The sides of the syrup are brought to the centre with the triangular knife with a rubbing motion (kneading), until the syrup turns white and starts to thicken. The syrup will now quickly set. Work it for a few minutes and seal in a container with lid.

~ Place the lukewarm syrup in the mixer, and blend until the syrup turns whitish and thick.

Note: for recipes with glucose the boiling point varies from 115°C (239°F) for soft fondant, to 118°C (244°F). The glucose content can vary from 10% to 20% of total sugars. Too little glucose can result in the sugar crystallising prematurely (not desirable). Too much glucose can result in the sugar syrup either not crystallising or doing so with great difficulty.

VARIATIONS /

CREAM FONDANT
1 kg sugar, 500 g cream (between 30 and 35% fat), 100 g glucose, 1 pinch of sodium bicarbonate, 116°C (241°F)
Proceed as in preceding recipes.

FRUIT FONDANT
1 kg sugar, 300 g water, 50 g glucose, 1 pinch of sodium bicarbonate, 150 à 200 g fruit paste, 116°C (241°F)

~ Bring sugar and water to the boil. Add glucose and continue to boil.
~ At approximately 110°C (230°F): add sodium bicarbonate.
~ At the end of the cooking process, add the preheated puree and continue to boil to 116°C (241°F).

Fudge

Fudge can best be described as a cross between caramel and fondant sugar. It is comparable to a crystallised, high quality, rich caramel. Put simply, to make fudge, start as for caramels and end as for fondant sugar.

Fudge recipes can differ a great deal: they must often be adapted to cooking conditions and finish. The range of ingredients used for caramels, can also be considered here.

SUGAR

The basic ingredient that leads to crystallisation.

GLUCOSE

The necessary supplement to sugar to limit its crystallisation and to provide the correct consistency to the liquid phase, just as with fondant sugar.

INVERT SUGAR OR SORBITOL

Like fondant sugar, fudge has a tendency to dry out rapidly due to its high relative humidity (70-75%). This tendency is even stronger if the fudge is lightened by adding frappé, whereby the moisture can evaporate more quickly. Adding moisture stabilisers, such as invert sugar or sorbitol, slows down the drying process.
The quantity of invert sugar to be added depends on the cooking speed, as during the heating process part of the sugar is converted into invert sugar. The disadvantage, however, to adding invert sugar is that it increases the fudge's sweet taste. Sorbitol on the other hand, tempers the sweetness, provides a finer granulometry and improves the softness and smoothness of the end product.

FAT

Lends softness to the fudge and prevents drying to some extent. Fat is required just as for caramels to provide a pleasant texture.

MILK PRODUCTS

Provide caramel flavour and colour.

FONDANT SUGAR

Seeding with fondant sugar is considerably better than with powdered sugar to start the fine crystal formation of the fudge. Adding powdered sugar gives the fudge a drier texture.

CREAM FUDGE

1,000 g sugar, 400 g cream, a pinch of sodium bicarbonate, 200 g butter

- Heat the sugar, cream and butter to 116°C (241°F).
- Leave to cool for 5 minutes.
- Mix syrup thoroughly with a spatula and rub regularly against the edge of the bowl, until the syrup loses its gloss and becomes slightly granular.
- Pour this mixture into a high rimmed Flexipan mould or onto an oiled baking sheet.
- Leave to cool until the fudge can be cut.

CHOCOLATE FUDGE

800 g sugar, 300 g milk, 1 vanilla pod, a pinch of sodium bicarbonate, 100 g butter, 100 g dark chocolate

- Bring the sugar, the milk and the vanilla pod to the boil.
- Add the butter and then the chocolate, and heat to 116°C (241°F).
- Leave to cool for 5 minutes and proceed as described above.

WHITE CHOCOLATE FUDGE

1,000 g sugar, 600 g cream, a pinch of sodium bicarbonate, 30 g butter, 240 g white chocolate

- Proceed as described above.

FUDGE USING ADDED FONDANT SUGAR AS SEED /

CARAMEL FUDGE

1,000 g sugar, 300 g water, 600 g glucose, 600 g sweetened condensed milk, 180 g butter, 4 g salt, a pinch of sodium bicarbonate, 120 g fondant sugar, vanilla

- Bring the sugar and water to the boil.
- Add glucose, sweetened condensed milk, butter, salt and sodium bicarbonate and continue to heat to 115-117°C (239-242.6°F).
- Put the boiled syrup in a mixer and mix gently while cooling. At approximately 100°C (212°F) the fondant sugar is added in small quantities until a homogeneous mass is obtained.
- Add flavourings.
- Pour in frame or mould and leave to cool.
- Cut and package.

CRYSTAL STRUCTURE IS TOO COARSE
- The syrup was kneaded too soon (too hot)
- The syrup was not kneaded enough
- The recipe contains too little moisture
- All sugar crystals must be dissolved before the syrup reaches its boiling point
- Stirring the syrup above its boiling point.

DISCOLORATION (DIRTY YELLOW)
- The syrup was cooked too slowly on an insufficient heat source.

TOO LITTLE FLAVOUR
- The flavourings were added too soon and were for the most part lost during cooking.

TOO SOFT
- Syrup temperature is too low
- An excessive percentage of fondant sugar was added to seed
- The syrup contains acids that slow down crystallisation
- The syrup was cooked too slowly on an insufficient heat source.

Sugar panning

Panning is enrobing all manner of nuts, dried fruits, chocolate items, etc., with a coat of chocolate, sugar in the form of microcrystals or various combinations of carbohydrates. For an attractive finish they are usually glazed or covered with a little silver or gold leaf. After this only dragées are coated with chocolate.

In order to be able to dip, a dipping kettle is a must. This is a turbine that can run at a variety of speeds and that can be set up in a controllable area.

Speeds must be adjustable from 18 to 24 revolutions per minute down to 8 to 10 revolutions per minute, depending on the product being dipped. The rounder and lighter the centres, the faster and more vertical the kettle should rotate; the heavier and more spiky the centres, the slower and more horizontal the kettle should

rotate. For chocolate dragées it is important to have an air-cooling system in place.

PRELIMINARY TREATMENT / **In order to be sugar coated, the products are first sifted to remove all impurities.** Then follows gumming with (depending on the centre):
- Gum arabic
- Gelatine
- Modified starch
- Maltodextrin

Gumming ensures better adherence of the centre and the sugar or chocolate coat and protects against drying or moisture absorption.

Pour a small quantity of gum on the products; start in the middle of the kettle and work outwards (between 8 to 15 ml per kg). L Allow the gum to spread over the products. After a few minutes cool dry air or fine sifted powdered sugar can be added. Do not run longer than necessary.

COATING WITH CHOCOLATE / **Add a sliver of warm chocolate between 38 and 40°C (100 to 104°F) radiating from the centre of the kettle outwards.** As a result of the constant movement the chocolate will start to adhere. Important: the products must stay in motion. As soon as everything is nicely coated with chocolate, cool air can be brought in. Another chocolate coat can

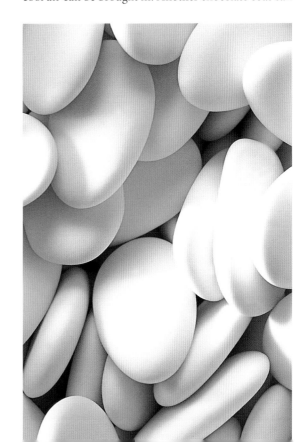

only be added when the first coat has crystallised. Repeat this process until the desired thickness is obtained. Coagulation problems could result from the following faults:

- Too much chocolate added at once
- The chocolate temperature is too low
- The kettle's rotation speed is too low

SUGAR COATING / **Heat 1 kg sugar and 300 gr water:**
- For big dragée centres to 110°C (230°F) = 77° Brix
- For small dragée centres to 105°C (221°F) = 67° Brix

BUFFING / **The panning kettle should be nice and smooth on the inside.** Return the dragées to the kettle. By introducing warm air the dragées' top chocolate coat will become slightly soft, which results in an attractive smooth product. Carefully remove the dragées from the kettle and let them crystallise on sheets for approximately twelve hours.

GLOSSING / **Gives an attractive appearance and protects against strange flavours and odours (extends shelf life).** Place the crystallised dragées in a panning kettle with an uneven lining. (Uneven lining can be created by spreading chocolate against the kettle sides and letting it harden.) Pour approximately 1/3 of the total gum quantity in a radiating fashion over the dragées and let them roll for a few minutes. Add cold air (approximately 18°C or 65°F) and allow to run for fifteen minutes. Repeat this process twice with the remaining gum.

VARNISHING / **Use 0.50 to 1% alcohol varnish.** Pour this in one go over the dragées and allow to run until they hardly stick. Turn the cool air on and let the dragées run at low speed until any alcohol odour has evaporated, otherwise the dragées could have a bitter taste.

DIPPING CANDIED FRUIT / **This is used in Middle Eastern countries in particular.**
Preferably use round fruit such as cherries.
The fruits are moistened in a panning kettle with sugar syrup that contains 0.2% invertase, to make them more even. Afterwards fondant powder is added to slightly dry the syrup and to enrobe the cherries with a fondant coat. This treatment will be repeated several times until the fondant coat around the cherries has the right thickness. After dipping with fondant the cherries are chocolate-coated in a clean dipping kettle. By enrobing the products later with chocolate undesirable leakage is prevented. Ideally the finished products are immediately packaged and kept for two weeks at a temperature of 20°C (68°F), to allow the invertase to give the fondant sugar a smooth texture.

[1] If you do not own a Baumé- or refractometer, you can use the following recipe: Add 2,700 gr sugar to 1,100 gr water, boil thoroughly for a few minutes and then cool.

[2] Osmosis: takes place when a liquid permeates a cell wall in one direction, if that wall separates two liquids for which it is permeable to different degrees.

[3] Angelica: is a forest plant of the parsley family from which oil is extracted, which serves as a basis for some medicines.

[4] Blanching: stops enzymatic changes and kills bacteria.

[5] Saturated: See section on "Caramelising".

[6] A little salt or sodium bicarbonate is often added to tone down the sweetness.

[7] Frappé: See "Miscellaneous" section.

Chocolate recipes based on nuts

Dulce de leche *85* / Praliné cream *86* / Raspberry praliné *89* /
Honey praliné cream *90* / Almond praliné *93* / Pistachio gianduja *94* /
Feuilletine *97* / Almond tuilles *98* /

Dulce de leche

Aw. 0,750

FOR THE BASE / 200 G PRALINÉ / 200 G GIANDUJA /
120 G MILK CHOCOLATE

500 G BUTTER / 350 G FONDANT SUGAR / 250 G MILK CHOCOLATE /
250 G DARK CHOCOLATE / 125 G DULCE DE LECHE COMPOUND
(AMORETTI NO. 396) / A PINCH OF POWDERED MACE/
A PINCH OF POWDERED BLACK PEPPER

Spread a thin coating of milk chocolate on baking paper. Immediately place a frame on the liquid chocolate. Mix the praliné with the precrystallised gianduja and milk chocolate, and pour into the frame (approximately 4 mm thick).

Whip the butter in a mixer and gradually add fondant sugar. Finally, mix both chocolates, flavourings and spices. Spread preparation on the gianduja mixture and allow to harden. Cut up with wire slicer. Dip into milk chocolate. Place a few nibs in the middle to garnish.

Praliné cream

Aw. 0,800

400 G WHIPPING CREAM / **400 G PRALINÉ (50/50)** /
500 G MILK CHOCOLATE / **NUTMEG POWDER**

Bring cream and nutmeg powder to the boil and pour onto the chopped chocolate. Blend in the praliné. Pour chocolate into moulds and allow chocolate to harden. Fill centre. Vibrate the moulds. Finish with chocolate.

Raspberry praliné

Aw. 0,564

200 G RASPBERRY PULP / **30 G SORBITOL** /
70 G WHIPPING CREAM / **200 G GIANDUJA** /
75 G WHITE CHOCOLATE / **OREGANO OIL EXTRACT (AMORETTI NO. 541)**

Bring the raspberry pulp, sorbitol and cream to the boil. Pour this mixture onto the finely chopped gianduja. Finally, add the extract, mix well and leave to cool. Fill chocolate moulds. After hardening off the chocolate shell, introduce the centre into the moulds. Allow to crust slightly and finish with chocolate.

Honey praliné cream

Aw. 0,588

100 G WHIPPING CREAM / 300 G HONEY / 250 G BUTTER /
400 G DARK CHOCOLATE / 400 G MILK CHOCOLATE /
600 G ALMOND PRALINÉ (SUCH AS PRAMA BY CALLEBAUT)

Combine butter, honey and almond praliné in mixer. Add the boiled cream.
Lastly fold in the chocolate.

Make round base from hard nougat or marzipan, or emboss round
gianduja or chocolate bases with rubber stencils (such as PCB. Ref. PRO 6A).
Pipe the centre onto bases in a ball shape. Allow to crystallise. Dip into milk
chocolate. Garnish.

Almond praliné

**150 G COARSELY GROUND ALMONDS / 40 G KIRSCH /
400 G ALMOND PRALINÉ / 100 G DARK CHOCOLATE /
150 G MILK CHOCOLATE**

Pour the kirsch onto the coarsely ground almonds and allow to stand for approximately 30 minutes. Combine the praliné with both chocolates. Add the almond chunks. Stir as little as possible and immediately pour the mixture into a frame on a Silpat baking mat. Apply a thin layer of dark chocolate over the top. Demould and turn over the product. Cut up with wire slicer or cut out with oval cutter.

If the almond chunks are mixed too thoroughly, the mass is likely to thicken and it will be difficult to smooth out the centre. If this occurs the centre should be rolled out between two levelling guides and two sheets of baking paper.

Pistachio gianduja

Aw. 0,792

800 G ALMONDS / **200 G PISTACHIO NUTS** /
800 G POWDERED SUGAR / **200 G COCOA BUTTER** /
400 G WHITE CHOCOLATE / **100 G PISTACHIO PASTE**

Roast the almonds. Grind the almonds, pistachio nuts and icing sugar into a fine dough in a food processor. Add cocoa butter, chocolate and pistachio paste, and blend into a homogeneous mixture. The mass must be pre-crystallised, before it is poured into a frame or onto a Silpat baking mat for rolling out.

White ganache

Aw. 0,876

300 G WHIPPING CREAM / **VANILLA** / **50 G CORN SYRUP** /
800 G WHITE CHOCOLATE / **100 G BUTTER**

Boil the cream with the corn syrup and pour onto the finely chopped chocolate. Allow mixture to cool to approximately 35°C (95°F), before adding the softened butter and vanilla. Pour the mixture onto the pistachio gianduja (approximately 4 mm thick). Allow to harden. De-mould and turn over the slab. Spread a thin coat of dark chocolate on the gianduja. After hardening turn over again and cut with wire slicer. Dip into dark chocolate. Garnish.

Feuilletine

600 G SUGAR / 750 G DARK GIANDUJA (SUCH AS CALLEBAUT GIAD2)

First method

Chop the gianduja into small pieces and pour into a mixing bowl. Melt the sugar until a light brown caramel is obtained. Pour the boiling caramel onto the gianduja and beat in a mixer until the mixture detaches from the edges of the bowl. Immediately pour onto a Silpat baking mat and roll out. Divide and cut immediately into desired shape. Leave to cool and dip into dark or milk chocolate. Garnish.

Second method

Heat the work surface on which the caramel will be poured using a sugar lamp. Bring the gianduja to a temperature of 45°C (113°F). Melt the sugar until a light caramel is obtained and pour the caramel onto a Silpat baking mat (which is placed on a warm surface). Pour gianduja over mixture and spread. Immediately fold ⅔ of the caramel slab closed using two triangular spatulas and fold over the remaining ⅓, thus creating three layers. Repeat in other direction.

Repeat several times (as with puff pastry) in order to produce thin flaky layers of caramel and gianduja. Roll out evenly to 1 cm thickness. Divide and cut immediately into desired shape. Leave to cool and dip into dark or milk chocolate. Garnish.

Almond tuilles

250 G SUGAR / **50 G WATER** / **200 G SHELLED ALMONDS** / **50 G HONEY** / **I KG MILK, WHITE OR DARK CHOCOLATE**

Crush almonds into pieces. Bring the sugar and water to the boil. Add the almonds to the syrup. Heat mixture while stirring until the syrup crystallises around the almonds and the mixture turns light brown.

Add honey and remove mixture from heat source. Pour onto a Silpat baking mat and leave to cool. Crush the grains into smaller grains and mix with precrystallised chocolate. Spread the mass in round stencils on strips of baking paper. Each strip should be draped over half round mould to harden after stencilling.

08

Fat-based recipes

Gingerbread cream *101* / Tropicana *102* / Butter praliné *105* /
Kahlua *106* / Egg yolk cream *109* / Arabe *110* /
Honey crunch *112* /

Gingerbread cream

Aw. 0,670

250 G BUTTER / **150 G PRALINÉ** /
GINGERBREAD SPICES / **450 G MILK CHOCOLATE**

Blend the spices thoroughly into the butter. Add the praliné and chocolate.
Pour dark chocolate into the moulds. After hardening, fill the chocolate
shells with the butter cream. After slight hardening, finish the moulds
with chocolate.

Tropicana

Aw. 0,744

300 G BUTTER / **300 G FONDANT SUGAR** /
750 G MELTED MILK CHOCOLATE / **100 G GRATED COCONUT** /
300 G BATIDA DE COCO (LIQUEUR)

Soak the grated coconut flakes in the liqueur. Whip the butter. Add the fondant sugar and continue to whip the mixture. Stir in the chocolate. Then add the coconut liqueur. Create round chocolate disks with a cutter. Pipe the butter ganache onto the bases with a fluted tip in a pointed peak. Allow to crust slightly. Dip into milk chocolate.

Butter praliné

Aw. 0,615

500 G BUTTER / **400 G LIQUID HONEY** / **400 G PRALINÉ** /
100 G CASSIS PUREE / **500 G WHITE CHOCOLATE** /
500 G MILK CHOCOLATE / **TURMERIC POWDER**

Soften butter and add honey and cassis puree. Fold in praliné and pre-crystallised chocolates. Add turmeric to taste. Fill mould, with shallow tubs, with a thin coat of dark or milk chocolate. After chocolate has hardened, shape centre into a ball with smooth decorating tip. Leave the semi-finished shells to cool. Demould carefully and allow to come to room temperature. Dip in the same chocolate as the tubs. Garnish.

Kahlua

250 G BUTTER / **500 G WHITE CHOCOLATE** / **50 G KAHLUA LIQUEUR**

Soften butter. Add precrystallised chocolate. Add liqueur to taste.

Stencil oval chocolate bases on a Silpat baking mat. Shape centre into an oval with smooth decorating tip. Allow the centres to crust. Dip the kahluas into dark chocolate. Garnish.

Egg yolk cream

Aw. 0,786

**300 G BUTTER / 200 G FONDANT SUGAR /
300 G EGG YOLK LIQUEUR (SEE P. 217) / 150 G WHITE CHOCOLATE**

Soften butter in a mixer. Add fondant sugar in small quantities. Fold in the white chocolate and then the liqueur. Pour the dark chocolate into a chocolate mould. Introduce the centre into the chocolate shells. Allow to crust slightly. Seal.

Arabe

Aw. 0,648

100 G PISTACHIO NUTS / **100 G MARZIPAN** / **100 G PASSOA LIQUEUR** /
30 G SORBITOL / **200 G LIQUID HONEY** / **300 G BUTTER** /
400 G WHITE CHOCOLATE / **400 G MILK CHOCOLATE**

Grind pistachio nuts into powder in food processor. Add marzipan and liqueur and mix thoroughly. Add honey and sorbitol and beat into a smooth cream. Remove centre from the cutter. Blend the softened butter with the centre. Fold in both chocolates.

Pour dark chocolate into a chocolate mould and allow to harden. Introduce centre into the shells and allow to stiffen slightly. Finish with dark chocolate.

Honey crunch

Aw. 0,713

140 G WILD HONEY / **50 G CORN SYRUP** / **250 G BUTTER** /
325 G DARK CHOCOLATE / **50 G CRUNCH**

FOR CRUNCH / **40 G ROASTED SESAME SEEDS** /
20 G DARK CHOCOLATE / **2 G TURMERIC**

For crunch blend mixture, spread thinly on Silpat baking mat and allow to harden. Grind to coarse grains in a blender.

Soften butter. Slightly heat the corn syrup and blend with honey. Add the crunch. Fold the precrystallised chocolate into the mixture. Fill the moulds and allow the chocolate to harden. Introduce centres into chocolate shells with a smooth decorating tip. Allow to crust slightly and seal with chocolate.

09

Ganaches

Ganache as a basic cream *120* / Piped nuts *121* / Hazelnut rosette *123* / Coffee Delight *124* /
Orange slices *127* / Cardamom and pistachio ganache *128* / Raspberry ganache *131* / Egg ganache with orange *132* /
Lemon *134* / Orient *135* / Gianduja ganache *137* / Mocha ganache *138* / Palet d'or *141* / Port *142* / Ganache with nutmeg praliné *144* /
Marquise *145* / Lava *146* / Saffron *149* / Coco Delight *150* / Marco *153* / Cappuccino *154* / Cream ganache with basil *156* /
Anise and honey ganache *157* / Relief palette *159* / Caramel snobinette *160* / Praliné ganache *163* / Tea ganache *164* /

Ganaches

Ganaches are velvety smooth chocolate creams and most are rich in fat. They are emulsions for which the main ingredients are always chocolate and a liquid.

The chocolate not only acts as a flavouring but, more importantly, determines the texture. Because of its high cocoa butter content it is best to use high-fat chocolate (couverture). For a high quality ganache a total fat content of approximately 40% is recommended. This is why cream is used as a liquid in most ganaches, although other liquids, such as infusions, coffee and liqueurs may also be used. In these cases the fat content must be complemented by adding butter or a vegetable fat. The chocolate quantity determines the consistency and can vary from 1,000 g whipping cream and 1,000 g chocolate to 1,000 g whipping cream and 4,000 g chocolate.

FOR EXAMPLE

1 part whipping cream to 1 part chocolate: very smooth creamy ganache. Can be used for moulding, but has very short shelf life.

1	1.5	Moulding. Piping on bases that are later dipped into chocolate.
1	2	Moulding. Piped truffles.
1	2.5	Can be cut with special cutter or knife.
1	3	Easy to cut.
1	4	Turns quite firm and dry.

SHELF LIFE / **The more chocolate is added, the firmer the centre and the longer the shelf life[1].** This is why increased chocolate doses are sometimes used. Dry cocoa components and sugar together with the liquid form a saturated solution. In it the sugar is able to crystallise within a short period of time. In order to prevent this and to improve the shelf life, without having to add a lot of chocolate, one or more moisture stabilisers can be added such as corn syrup[2] (in particular corn syrup with a high DE value) or invert sugar, honey, sorbitol, etc. Part of the water can also be replaced with fat, for example: substitute part of the cream with butter (whipping cream contains approximately 60% water, butter a mere 18%). As long as the emulsion is not disturbed, the ganache can be improved by adding butter, fruit puree, liqueurs, etc. Hygienic working practices and the use of high-quality ingredients are an absolute must.

PRECRYSTALLISING / **All ganaches must be precrystallised in order to produce fat crystallisation that is as fine and as smooth as possible.** Precrystallised ganache is finer in texture, tastes better and remains stable for longer. Cooled ganache that is not precrystallised, may curdle more quickly. Precrystallising: whilst stirring leave to cool as quickly as possible, until the desired consistency is reached. Precrystallised ganache that is later stirred to make it easier to introduce, has a different organoleptic feel and taste, and may curdle in some recipes. Stirring introduces air into the ganache. Because of the oxygen present in the air, fats oxidise (milk fat and cocoa butter), and this will rapidly change the flavour. The microbiological decay in the air is introduced into the ganache, and this deteriorates flavour and shelf life more quickly. Stirring, if at all necessary, is to be kept to a minimum. Ganaches for the glazing of cakes are best homogenised, in order to obtain extra fine fat distribution, which improves gloss.

CURDLING (SEE P. 116) / **Is the separation of an emulsion from two liquid substances that do not form a solution.** The most typical example is oil and water (mayonnaise).
Causes:
- Incorrect balance of ingredients
- Incorrect mixing temperatures
- Chocolate PH too low
Remedies: (depending on recipe)
- Homogenise with blender
- Add emulsifier (in some cases a little lecithin helps)
- Add a thickener
- Allow to solidify slightly, then stir vigorously (possibly in beater/mixer).

GANACHES WITH LONG SHELF LIFE / **If hygiene rules are observed correctly during preparation and stora-**

ge, these (industrial) ganaches can remain free of bacterial contamination for up to one year. Basic principle when making such ganaches: Sugar syrup of at least 75° Brix to which (stable) ingredients are added to determine consistency, structure and (stable) flavourings.

FOR EXAMPLE

Chocolate: dark, milk or white chocolate. Preferably poor on cocoa butter chocolat to limit impact on firmness (the more chocolate, the firmer and harder the structure). In order to enhance the chocolate flavour, cocoa powder may be added to the mixture. Safflower or sunflower oil could also be folded into the chocolate to change the texture. Various flavourings and liqueur concentrates may also be added.

The recipes below are quite flexible; they cannot be compared with classic ganache recipes with a shelf life of only one to two months. They should therefore be adapted in accordance with requirements and as indicated above.

RECIPE I   AW. 0,690

Basic syrup: 500 g sugar, 150 g water,
450 g corn syrup 55 DE, 230 g sweetened condensed milk
  - Bring the sugar and water to the boil.
  - Add the corn syrup and heat to 75° Brix, i.e. 115°C (239°F).

  - Add sweetened condensed milk.
  - Leave to cool to less than 40°C (104°F).

RECIPE 2   AW. 0,660

Basic syrup: 200 g sugar, 100 g water, 100 g whipping cream, 150 g butter, 250 g corn syrup 55 DE, 18 g sorbitol powder
  - Bring sugar, water, cream and butter to the boil.
  - Add the corn syrup and then the sorbitol.
  - Heat mixture to 75° Brix.
  - Leave mixture to cool to less than 40°C (104°F).
  - Blend 200 g of this basic syrup with 50 g milk chocolate.
  - Add flavourings and/or liqueur concentrate.

RECIPE 3   AW. 0,650

400 g condensed milk, sodium bicarbonate,
10 g sorbitol, 120 g corn syrup, 1,000 g chocolate,
200 g invert sugar, 60 g alcohol (flavouring to taste)
  - Bring milk, sodium bicarbonate and corn syrup to the boil.
  - Add sorbitol and heat mixture to 75° Brix.
  - Pour mixture onto the chocolate and fold in invert sugar.
  - Finally add alcohol and flavourings to taste.

RECIPE 4   AW. 0,640

500 g sugar, 150 g water, 440 g corn syrup 55 DE, 130 g invert sugar, 230 g sweetened condensed milk, 3 g sodium bicarbonate, 10 g sorbitol
  - Bring the sugar and water to the boil.
  - Add corn syrup, invert sugar, sweetened condensed milk, sodium bicarbonate and sorbitol, and heat mixture to 75° Brix.

Warning! At high temperatures invert sugar strongly discolours and gives off a caramel taste. Preferably use a large saucepan since the mixture foams due to the blending of sodium bicarbonate and sorbitol, and may boil over.

RECIPE 5   AW. 0,593

750 g sugar, 325 g water, 250 g corn syrup, 200 g oil,
800 g chocolate, 400 g invert sugar
  - Melt the sugar into caramel.
  - As soon as the sugar turns golden brown, carefully quench with water.
  - Add the corn syrup.

EBAUT   CA

~ Mix the oil and chocolate, stir into the syrup and add the invert sugar.

RECIPE 6   AW. 0,607
750 g sugar, 325 g water, 200 g corn syrup, 600 g chocolate, 200 g invert sugar
~ Melt the sugar into caramel.
~ As soon as the sugar turns golden brown, carefully quench with water.
~ Add the corn syrup.
~ Add the chocolate and then the invert sugar.

Butter ganache

The main ingredients for this ganache are butter and chocolate. The butter replaces the cream, which considerably reduces the moisture content compared to classic ganache. Whipping cream contains approximately 60 to 65% water, butter a mere 18%. This means that butter ganache has a longer shelf life. The melting point of butter, which is around 27°C (80.6°F), provides a pleasant creamy texture. As with regular ganache the shelf life can be increased by adding moisture stabilisers. See 'Water activity' in the section on 'Factors that extend shelf life' and 'Characteristics of the most frequently used ingredients'.

Because of their smooth texture, these butter creams are often easy to pipe into moulds or onto a Silpat baking mat, as for truffles. The chocolate quantity largely determines the flavour, but the cocoa butter in the chocolate gives the butter ganache body and firmness. Due to the quantity of milk fats in milk chocolate, more chocolate is added when using milk chocolate, to obtain the same consistency as when using dark chocolate. If white chocolate is used, even more chocolate will have to be added. The shelf life can also be somewhat extended by increasing the quantity of chocolate.

[1] See Water activity in the section on 'Factors that extend shelf life'.

[2] See section on 'Characteristics of the most frequently used ingredients'.

Ganache as a basic cream

Aw. 0,751

In order to save time, many chocolatiers who are just starting production, make a few basic creams. These are then divided into two or more parts, and each part will be given a different taste, consistency, appearance and finish.

800 G SUGAR / 500 G WATER / 400 G SWEETENED MILK /
1,500 G CORN SYRUP / 200 G INVERT SUGAR /
3,000 G BUTTER / 4,000 G DARK CHOCOLATE

Bring the sugar, water, sweetened condensed milk and corn syrup to the boil. Leave to stand until lukewarm and add invert sugar. Leave the sugar to cool completely. Whip the butter and slowly pour the cooled syrup onto the butter while the machine is running. Quickly fold in chocolate that is slightly too warm (approx. 35°C or 95°F).

Piped nuts

Combine the marzipan with pistachio flavouring and roll out the mixture to a thickness of 3 mm. Cut out oval bases and arrange them on baking paper.

Flavour a basic ganache with 60% kirsch. With the help of a no. 8 even decorating tip, pipe sphere-shaped ovals onto the marzipan bases. Garnish immediately with half a walnut. Allow the centres to crust slightly before dipping into milk chocolate. Garnish.

Hazelnut rosette

Flavour a basic ganache with vanilla. Shape thin round bases of dark chocolate on baking paper. Allow to harden. With the help of a serrated decorating tip, pipe double rosettes onto the chocolate bases. Immediately place a roasted hazelnut on the ganache, pointed side up. Leave to crust slightly. Dip ⅔ of the hazelnut rosette into dark chocolate.

Coffee Delight

Spread dark chocolate on a stencil with oval cut-outs (such as PCB no. PO 01A), on baking paper.

If you do not have an oval stencil: Spread a thin layer of dark chocolate on baking paper. Before the chocolate is fully hardened, cut out oval shapes with an oval cutter. Stick the shapes to the baking paper with the help of a cone of dark chocolate.

Combine 1 kg basic ganache with 15 to 20 g finely ground fresh coffee and 50 g dark chocolate. Immediately pipe the mixture with a serrated decorating tip no. 5 in an upward motion to form an S-shape. Leave to crust slightly and dip the delight into dark chocolate to ⅔ of its height.

Orange slices

1,000 G BASIC GANACHE (SEE P. 115) / 100 G DARK CHOCOLATE /
150 G CANDIED ORANGE PEEL / SOME COINTREAU (OPTIONAL)

Finely chop the candied orange peel. Pour some Cointreau onto the peel to prevent the fruit from sticking to the knife. Allow the liqueur to penetrate. Mix the chocolate with the basic ganache and add the chopped peel. Scoop up half a level tablespoon of the mixture and use index finger to shape it into an S on baking paper. Allow the shapes to harden and dip them into dark chocolate.

Cardamom and pistachio ganache

200 G WHIPPING CREAM / 25 G PISTACHIO COMPOUND
(E.G. AMORETTI NO. 5) / 400 G DARK CHOCOLATE /
50 G INVERT SUGAR / 200 G WHIPPING CREAM /
8 G CARDAMOM POWDER / 500 G WHITE CHOCOLATE

Pour the lukewarm cream onto the tempered chocolate. Add invert sugar and pistachio compound. Mix thoroughly. Pour the mixture into a frame on baking paper or a 'feuille guitare' and allow to harden slightly.

Bring the cream and cardamom to the boil. Allow to stand. Pour mixture onto the white chocolate and stir until ganache is smooth. Pour the pre-crystallised ganache onto the first layer in a frame, up to a total height of 1 cm. Allow to harden and cut with wire slicer. Dip into dark chocolate. Garnish.

Raspberry ganache

Aw. 0,788

600 G RASPBERRY PUREE / 160 G SUGAR / 300 G WHIPPING CREAM /
150 G INVERT SUGAR / 2,000 G DARK CHOCOLATE /
100 G BUTTER / 80 G FRAMBOISE JACOBERT

Moulding

Leave puree and sugar to boil for a few minutes. Meanwhile, bring the
cream to the boil. Blend the cream with the puree and immediately pour
onto finely chopped chocolate. Add the liqueur and invert sugar. Next add
butter. Pour chocolate moulds and allow chocolate to harden. Introduce
centres into shells using smooth decorating tip. Leave to crust slightly and
finish with chocolate.

As a cutting praline

This centre can also be used for a cutting praline (requires 2,200 g chocolate). Pour the centre into a frame and leave to harden. Demould. Spread a
thin layer of chocolate on the surface. After hardening turn the slab upside
down. Cut with wire slicer. Dip the pieces into milk chocolate. Garnish.

Egg ganache with orange

Aw. 0,784

6 EGGS / **200 G SUGAR** / **200 G WHIPPING CREAM** / **200 G BUTTER** /
100 G ORANGE JUICE / **RIND FROM TWO ORANGES** /
100 G INVERT SUGAR / **1,100 G CHOPPED DARK CHOCOLATE**

Bring sugar, cream, butter, orange juice and rind to the boil. Lightly beat the eggs. Pour the mixture onto the eggs and reheat to approximately 80°C (176°F). Stir thoroughly! Pour the mixture onto the chopped chocolate.

Spread the mixture in a frame on baking paper or on a 'feuille guitare' (1 cm thick). Leave to harden overnight. Demould and spread thin layer of milk chocolate on the slab. Turn it over and divide into squares with wire slicer. Dip the pieces into milk chocolate. Garnish.

Lemon

Aw. 0,786

**300 G WHIPPING CREAM / 100 G CORN SYRUP /
600 G WHITE CHOCOLATE / 200 G MILK CHOCOLATE /
150 G PRALINÉ / 150 G BUTTER / 100 G MYCRYO COCOA BUTTER /
LEMON COMPOUND (SUCH AS AMORETTI NO. 304)**

Bring cream and corn syrup to the boil and pour onto the chopped white and milk chocolate. Add the praliné to this ganache, then the butter and finally the compound. Leave the mixture to cool to 40°C before adding the Mycryo cocoa butter. If Mycryo cocoa butter is not used, the melted cocoa butter must be precrystallised.

Whip the mixture. Pipe bars of approximately 10 mm diameter onto baking paper and allow to harden. Brush chocolate on top of the bars. Cut with wire slicer. Dip the pieces in milk chocolate and garnish.

Orient

Aw. 0,560

650 G WHIPPING CREAM / **30 G GREEN TEA** /
5 G FRESH MINT LEAVES / **50 G CORN SYRUP** /
500 G DARK CHOCOLATE / **700 G MILK CHOCOLATE** /
60 G INVERT SUGAR / **100 G BUTTER**

Bring cream, corn syrup, green tea and mint leaves to the boil, and allow to stand for five minutes. Sieve the mixture and add the invert sugar. Combine with tempered chocolates and immediately add the softened butter. Pour the mixture into a frame to a thickness of approximately 12 mm and allow to harden.

After demoulding spread a thin layer of dark chocolate on the surface and allow to harden. Turn the slab over and cut with cutting frame. Dip the pieces into dark chocolate.

Gianduja ganache

Aw. 0,705

250 G WHIPPING CREAM / 300 G GIANDUJA /
350 G MILK CHOCOLATE / 60 G HONEY /
100 G BUTTER (AT ROOM TEMPERATURE) / VANILLA

Boil the cream and pour it over the gianduja and milk chocolate. Add the honey and bring the mixture to a temperature of approximately 36°C (97°F) before folding in the butter. Pour the ganache onto a Silpat baking mat in a frame and allow to crystallise overnight.

Demould and spread a thin layer of milk chocolate on the slab. Turn the slab over and cut with wire slicer. Dip the ganaches into milk chocolate. Garnish.

Mocha ganache

Aw. 0,751

**400 G WHIPPING CREAM / 50 G CORN SYRUP /
40 G FINELY GROUND COFFEE / 1,200 G MILK CHOCOLATE /
60 G INVERT SUGAR / 200 G BUTTER**

Bring cream, corn syrup and coffee to the boil and pour the liquid onto the melted chocolate. Blend in the invert sugar. As soon as the centre has reached a temperature of approximately 30°C (86°F), add to butter. Spread the mixture in a frame. After hardening, cover the slab with a thin coating of dark chocolate. Demould, turn over the slab and cut with wire slicer or remove disks of approximately 25 mm diameter with a round cutter. Dip the ganaches into dark chocolate. Garnish.

Palet d'or

Palet d'or is originally a French recipe. This little gem is often round, has a flat and very glossy surface, and is decorated in gold. A Palet d'or is made from classic ganache that is often enriched with butter.

Aw. 0,871 / **650 G WHIPPING CREAM** /
1,800 G DARK CHOCOLATE 70% / **300 G BUTTER** / **50 G CORN SYRUP**

Aw. 0,877 / **1,300 G WHIPPING CREAM** /
2,000 G DARK CHOCOLATE 70% / **300 G BUTTER**

Aw. 0,880 / **500 G WHIPPING CREAM** /
DARK CHOCOLATE 70% / **100 G INVERT SUGAR** / **100 G BUTTER**

Procedure with UHT cream
Heat UHT cream (and possibly corn syrup) to approximately 35°C (95°F). Add the tempered chocolate and stir until a smooth mass is obtained. If required add invert sugar. Finally fold in the butter brought to room temperature.

Procedure with fresh cream
Bring cream (and possibly corn syrup) to the boil and pour onto finely chopped chocolate. Add invert sugar (where indicated) and stir until a smooth mass is obtained. Combine the butter brought to room temperature with the ganache, when the latter has reached a temperature of approximately 40°C (104°F). Pour into a frame (to a thickness of 10 mm). Allow to solidify and demould. Spread a thin coat of chocolate onto the base. Cut out disks with a diameter of approximately 2.5 cm. Dip disks into 70% dark chocolate. Immediately apply shiny foil to the surface. Allow to crystallise for a few hours before removing foil. Garnish with golden nugget.

Port

Aw. 0,796

400 G WHIPPING CREAM / **100 G SUGAR** /
100 G EGG YOLK / **200 G PORT** / **700 G MILK CHOCOLATE** /
500 G DARK CHOCOLATE / **50 G BUTTER**

For moulded pralines
Bring ⅔ of the cream to the boil. Combine the sugar with the egg yolk and fold into ⅓ of the cream. Mix and bring to the boil until mixture binds. Remove from heat. Add port and then chocolate, and finally the butter. Fill moulds with chocolate of your choice and allow shells to harden. Introduce centres into chocolate shells with smooth decorating tip. Allow to slightly crust. Seal with chocolate.

For cutting pralines
For cutting pralines the quantity of milk chocolate is increased to 900 g. Pour the mixture into a frame (to a thickness of 10 mm). Allow to harden overnight. After demoulding, cover the slab with a thin coating of dark chocolate. Turn the slab upside down and cut with cutter. Dip the pieces into dark chocolate. Garnish immediately.

Ganache with nutmeg praliné

Aw. 0,734

600 G WHIPPING CREAM / **20 G INSTANT COFFEE** / **PINCH OF NUTMEG** / **600 G PRALINÉ** / **70 G HONEY** / **1,000 G MILK CHOCOLATE**

FOR BASES AND COVERS / **100 G ROASTED SESAME SEEDS** / **170 G MILK CHOCOLATE**

First prepare the bases and covers. Blend the roasted sesame seeds and the precrystallised milk chocolate. Pour the chocolate onto a Silpat baking mat and spread mixture out thinly. After hardening cut out a sufficient number of disks for the bases and covers of the pralines.

Bring cream, instant coffee and nutmeg to the boil, and pour this mixture onto the praliné. Fold in honey together with precrystallised chocolate. Combine into a nice homogeneous mass. Pipe centres in a ball onto the bases and add the covers. Ensure that covers are horizontal by gently pressing them with a flat plate after piping. Dip the ganaches into the chocolate of your choice. Finish with a fork stroke.

Marquise

**1,000 G BASIC CARAMEL CREAM (SEE BASIC CARAMEL CREAM IN THE
SECTION ON 'CARAMEL SYRUPS AND CREAMS', P. 75)** /
1,000 G WHITE OR MILK CHOCOLATE /
A DASH OF COINTREAU

Combine the chocolate with the caramel cream. (The centre will tend to
curdle.) Cool the mixture immediately and leave to partially crystallise.
Whisk centres in mixer and flavour with Cointreau. If the cream is still a
little too firm, the edges of the mixing bowl should be slightly heated while
the mixer is running.

Pour dark chocolate into the moulds. Leave the shells to harden and fill
with caramel cream. Leave to crust slightly. Finish with chocolate. Vibrate
thoroughly to remove air bubbles and place in cooling substance.

Lava

Aw. 0,826

300 G WHIPPING CREAM / **50 G INVERT SUGAR** /
500 G DARK CHOCOLATE / **100 G BUTTER** /
MACE / **GRATED LEMON RIND**

Bring the cream and mace to the boil. Pour this mixture onto the finely chopped chocolate. Add the invert sugar and grated lemon rind. Leave to cool to approximately 30°C (86°F) and add the butter. Pour the mixture into a frame (to a thickness of 12 mm). Leave to harden sufficiently, before demoulding. Apply a thin coat of chocolate. Turn the slab upside down and apply a coat of chocolate on this side as well.

Draw a wavy shape using a garnishing comb as soon as the chocolate thickens slightly. Immediately cut with a wire slicer to the desired size. Dip the pieces into dark chocolate up to the edges.

Saffron

Aw. 0,786

300 G WHIPPING CREAM / **40 G CORN SYRUP** / **SAFFRON** /
850 G MILK CHOCOLATE / **40 G INVERT SUGAR** / **70 G BUTTER**

Bring cream, corn syrup and saffron to the boil and allow to set for five minutes. Add the invert sugar and pour the cream through a sieve onto the precrystallised chocolate. Add the softened butter. Pour into a frame (to a thickness of 8 to 10 mm). Leave to harden. Demould the slab and apply a thin coat of dark chocolate. After hardening turn the slab over and cut with wire slicer. Dip the pieces into dark chocolate.

Coco Delight

Aw. 0,829

250 G COCONUT MILK / **500 G WHITE CHOCOLATE** /
50 G MYCRYO COCOA BUTTER / **30 G INVERT SUGAR** /
200 G GRATED COCONUT / **TANGERINE COMPOUND (AMORETTI NO. 306)**

Bring the coconut milk to the boil and add the grated chocolate. Add the invert sugar and the grated coconut and lastly the compound. Leave to cool to 40°C (104°F) and add the Mycryo cocoa butter. (If Mycryo cocoa butter is not used, allow the filling to reach room temperature and fold in the tempered cocoa butter). Spread in a frame and allow to harden. Cut with a cutter. Dip the pieces into dark chocolate. Garnish.

Note:
If this item is dipped into dark chocolate, extra attention must be paid to storage, otherwise fat bloom may occur quite rapidly (see section on 'Fat bloom'). To ensure a long shelf life it is recommended that this item be dipped into dark coloured milk chocolate (a mixture of 50% milk and 50% dark chocolate).

Marco

Aw. 0,754

800 G WHIPPING CREAM / 1,100 G WHITE CHOCOLATE /
300 G MILK CHOCOLATE / 150 G BUTTER /
300 G MARZIPAN 1/1 / 200 G COGNAC

Bring the cream to the boil and pour it onto the finely chopped chocolate. Combine the marzipan with the cognac. Add butter to the marzipan mixture. Blend well. Pour dark chocolate into a mould. After hardening, introduce centres into chocolate shells using smooth decorating tip. Leave to crust slightly and finish with dark chocolate.

Cappuccino

Aw. 0,745

250 G SUGAR / 500 G WHIPPING CREAM /
1,000 G CAPPUCCINO CHOCOLATE (CALLEBAUT) / 100 G BUTTER

Caramelise sugar. Add cream and quickly bring to the boil. Fold in the chopped cappuccino chocolate. After cooling, add the softened butter. Lightly whip mixture in a mixer. Spread the mixture in a frame and leave to harden overnight.

Demould and cover the top of the slab with a thin layer of milk chocolate. Turn upside down and cut up with wire slicer. Dip the pieces into milk chocolate and garnish immediately.

Cream ganache with basil

Aw. 0,785

1,100 G WHIPPING CREAM / **240 G CORN SYRUP** /
DRIED AND POWDERED BASIL / **2,300 G MILK CHOCOLATE** /
100 G BUTTER / **100 G INVERT SUGAR**

Bring the cream and corn syrup to the boil. Add the basil powder and allow to stand for five minutes[1]. Sieve the mixture and pour it over the chopped chocolate. Add the invert sugar and then the butter. Leave to cool. Fill a chocolate mould. After hardening of the chocolate shell, introduce the centre into the moulds. Leave to crust slightly and finish the ganaches with chocolate.

[1] Do not boil the basil, but add at the end.

Anise and honey ganache

Aw. 0,802

350 G WHIPPING CREAM / **10 G ANISE** / **50 G HONEY** /
500 G MILK CHOCOLATE / **100 G BUTTER**

Bring the cream and anise to the boil and allow to simmer for a few minutes. Pour the cream mixture through a strainer onto the chocolate. Fold in the honey. Leave until lukewarm and add butter.

Pour the chocolate into moulds in the shape of half bullets. Once solidified use a palette knife to spread the ganache in the chocolate shells. Immediately hold the moulds sideways so as to be able to remove some of the centre. Smoothen the moulds. Allow to solidify slightly and finish with chocolate. Demould. Dip into milk or dark chocolate. Garnish.

Relief palette

Aw. 0,801

420 G WHIPPING CREAM / **850 G DARK CHOCOLATE** /
50 G INVERT SUGAR / **170 G BUTTER**

Bring the cream to the boil and pour it onto the finely chopped chocolate.
Blend in the invert sugar. Fold in the softened butter as soon as the ganache
is lukewarm. Pour the mixture into a frame and allow to harden overnight.
Demould the slab. Cover the surface with a thin layer of dark chocolate
and allow to harden. Turn over the slab and cut up with wire slicer. Dip the
pieces into chocolate and immediately apply relief foil (to garnish). Leave
to harden for at least one hour before removing the foil.

Caramel snobinette

Moulds for this praline can be home made and reused. Cut our circles from foam rubber. Wrap the circles in very thin and flexible foil[1]. Seal the foil at the top. Dip the moulds into precrystallised dark chocolate up to ⅔ height and arrange on a Silpat baking mat or on baking paper. Allow the chocolate to harden. Demould by squeezing the foam rubber and by gently removing the mould from the chocolate tub using a twisting motion.

1,000 G BASIC CARAMEL CREAM (SEE BASIC CARAMEL CREAM IN THE SECTION ON 'CARAMEL SYRUPS AND CREAMS', P. 75) /
300 G WHITE OR MILK CHOCOLATE / **COFFEE PASTE**

Combine the chocolate with the caramel cream and add the coffee flavour. Immediately fill the chocolate tubs with the caramel cream up to 3 mm from the top edge, using a pastry bag. Make milk chocolate extra liquid by adding a little melted cocoa butter. Finish snobinettes and slightly vibrate the plate in order to even out the tubs.

[1] Ideal is to use the type of foil used by supermarkets to wrap fruit and vegetables.

Praliné ganache

Aw. 0,816

500 G WHIPPING CREAM / **100 G CORN SYRUP** / **500 G PRALINÉ** /
300 G MILK CHOCOLATE / **100 G DARK CHOCOLATE** /
BLACK PEPPER /

Combine the praliné with the chocolate. Bring the cream and the corn syrup to the boil and add to praliné mixture. Leave to cool. Fill the moulds and allow the chocolate to harden. Introduce centres into chocolate shells using smooth decorating tip. Leave to crust slightly. Seal with chocolate.

Tea ganache

Aw. 0,808

**80 G BLACK TEA / 2,500 G WHIPPING CREAM /
600 G INVERT SUGAR / 600 G BUTTER (AT ROOM TEMPERATURE) /
60 G ORANGE BLOSSOM WATER / BRANDY ST. REMY (OPTIONAL) /
3,000 G MILK CHOCOLATE**

Bring the cream and tea to the boil. Allow to simmer for a few minutes. Sieve. Add the butter, invert sugar, orange blossom water and, if desired, the St. Remy brandy to the cream. Combine with the precrystallised chocolate. Fill the moulds and allow the chocolate to harden. Introduce centres into shells using smooth decorating tip. Leave to crust slightly and seal with chocolate.

For cut pralines 4,000 g of milk chocolate is required. Pour the mixture into a frame on a Silpat baking mat and leave to harden. Spread a thin layer of chocolate on the surface. After hardening turn over the slab and cut up with wire slicer. Dip the tea ganaches into dark chocolate and garnish.

10

Caramels

Butter caramels *167* / Nut caramels *168* / Honey caramels *170* / Chocolate caramels *171* / Black Devils *173* / Caramel bites *174* /

Butter caramels

Three versions

1,000 G SUGAR / 875 G WHIPPING CREAM / 500 G CORN SYRUP / 250 G BUTTER / VANILLA EXTRACT

1,000 G SUGAR / 2,000 G MILK / 1,000 G CORN SYRUP / 400 G BUTTER / VANILLA EXTRACT

1,000 G SUGAR / 200 G MILK POWDER / 500 G WATER / 600 G CORN SYRUP / 500 G BUTTER / VANILLA EXTRACT

Bring sugar, liquid and corn syrup to the boil. Brush the edges of a bowl with water to remove all undesirable crystals. Add the butter once the temperature of the mixture exceeds 112°C (235°F). Add the vanilla only when the desired temperature is nearly reached. At the cooking temperature pour the mixture onto a Silpat baking mat in a frame and leave to cool.

Cut the mixture as soon as it has reached the desired firmness, wrap immediately or dip into chocolate. (Only cut with a knife and in a sawing motion to prevent the caramel from sticking to the knife.)

Nut caramels

All kinds of nuts can be used to make nut caramels. Preference is given to walnuts, hazelnuts, pecan nuts, pistachios and macadamia nuts. Sesame, sunflower or pumpkin seeds are also used.

Three versions

1,000 G SUGAR / 500 G CORN SYRUP / 250 G MILK /
500 G WHIPPING CREAM / 125 G BUTTER / 1,000 G CHOPPED NUTS

1,000 G SUGAR / 600 G WHIPPING CREAM / 600 G CORN SYRUP /
150 G BUTTER / 500 G CHOPPED NUTS / VANILLA EXTRACT

500 G SUGAR / 200 G CORN SYRUP / 500 G WHIPPING CREAM /
300 G CHOCOLATE / 400 G BUTTER / 400 G CHOPPED NUTS

Melt the corn syrup, add sugar and heat until the mixture turns into caramel. Add the milk and cream. Heat to the desired cooking point, add the butter and possibly the chocolate or vanilla. Fold in the nuts. Pour the mixture into a frame on a Silpat baking mat. Leave to cool and cut when mixture reaches the desired firmness.

Honey caramels

500 G SUGAR / 500 G HONEY / 500 G WHIPPING CREAM /
250 G BUTTER / SOME LAVENDER OIL OR FLAVOURING (OPTIONAL)

Bring sugar, honey and cream to the boil. Brush the edges of a bowl with water to remove all undesirable crystals. Add the butter once the temperature of the mixture exceeds 112°C (235°F). Bring to the desired cooking point and, if required, add lavender oil or flavouring. Pour onto a Silpat baking mat and leave to cool. Leave the caramel to cool. Cut when desired firmness is obtained.

Chocolate caramels

1,000 G SUGAR / **500 G WHIPPING CREAM** /
500 G CORN SYRUP / **100 G BUTTER** /
100 TO 150 G BLOCK CHOCOLATE OF 100 G COCOA MASS

Bring sugar, cream and corn syrup to the boil. Carefully brush the edges of the bowl with water. Add the butter once the temperature of the mixture hovers around 110°C (230°F). Add the chocolate. Bring to desired cooking point. Pour the mixture into a frame on a Silpat baking mat. Cut when desired firmness is obtained. Wrap immediately or dip into chocolate.

Black Devils

Black devils are chocolate caramels, often made from rejected pralines.

1,000 G SUGAR / **300 G WATER** / **600 G CORN SYRUP** /
150 G COCOA POWDER / **150 G BUTTER**

Bring milk, water and corn syrup to the boil. Brush the edges of a bowl with water in order to prevent any undesirable crystallisation. Melt the butter and carefully fold in cocoa powder, until all cocoa lumps are dissolved. Add the cocoa mixture to the syrup when it reaches approximately 110°C (230°F), and continue to heat to the desired cooking point. (See 'Caramels'.) Pour the mixture into a frame on a Silpat baking mat. Leave to cool sufficiently and cut. Wrap the devils immediately or dip into chocolate.

Points of particular interest when processing rejected chocolates
- Processing marzipan or mint is out of the question.
- In order to boil sugar all that is required is to melt 300 g water on 1,000 g sugar. Using more makes no sense, since the mixture has to boil to achieve the desired cooking point.
- Melting chocolates requires more water, in order to avoid scorching.
- At least 50% corn syrup must be added to the total sugar quantity.

Once the chocolates contain a sufficient amount of the various required ingredients to be able to form caramels (sugar, corn syrup, fat and chocolate), it is easy to create new recipes. The following recipe produces good results, provided the aforementioned points are taken into account:

2,000 G CHOCOLATES FOR REPROCESSING / **700 G WATER** /
2 G SODIUM BICARBONATE / **500 G SUGAR (IF REQUIRED)** / **500 G CORN SYRUP** /
BUTTER (IF PRALINES DO NOT CONTAIN BUTTER) / **VANILLA EXTRACT**

Slowly heat the pralines, water and sodium bicarbonate. Stir well to avoid scorching. At the boiling point, strain the mixture. Add the sugar and corn syrup and continue to boil. At approximately 110°C (230°F) add fat. Add the vanilla a few degrees before the desired cooking point is reached. Pour the mixture into a frame on a Silpat baking mat. Leave to cool before cutting. Wrap immediately or dip into chocolate.

Caramel bites

1,000 G SUGAR / 400 G CONDENSED MILK /
300 G ROASTED AND CRUSHED HAZELNUTS /
10 G COFFEE FLAVOURING / A DASH OF SODIUM BICARBONATE /
800 G MILK CHOCOLATE (IN WARM WEATHER: 1,000 G)

Heat the milk and the sodium bicarbonate. Melt the sugar until carameli-sation occurs. Gradually add the milk to the caramel, whilst stirring thoroughly. Blend in the hazelnut pieces and coffee flavouring, and finally the chocolate. Pour the mixture onto a Silpat baking mat and leave to stand overnight. Roll out the mixture to 12 mm and cut using a knife. Dip the bites into milk chocolate. Garnish.

II

Nougat

There are innumerable recipes for nougat: soft, hard, with or without fruit, with nuts or chocolate, etc. The same principle applies to all recipes, i.e. good nougat must be light and should not stick, run or crystallise.

EFFECTS OF THE MOST FREQUENTLY USED INGREDIENTS IN THE MAKING OF NOUGAT /

- Honey[1]: slows down crystallisation and gives a pleasant taste.
- Corn syrup: slows down crystallisation and replaces part of the honey if too expensive.
- Sugar: makes nougat firm and dry.
- Egg whites: render nougat light and reduce the sweetness of the nougat.
- Fat: It is recommended to add a little fat, especially for nougat that contains little dried fruit, in order to prevent the nougat from sticking to the teeth.

VARIOUS WORKING METHODS /

WORKING METHOD 1

1,000 g sugar, 300 g water, 1,000 g honey, 8 egg whites, vanilla or orange blossom water, 2,000 g almonds, 200 g pistachio nuts
- Roast the almonds until golden brown.
- Boil the sugar, water and honey to 125°C (257°F). Meanwhile beat the egg whites until stiff and pour the sugar syrup onto it in a spiral.
- Heat the edges of the mixing bowl with a heat gun to dry the mixture, until the nougat no longer sticks to the back of the hand.
- Replace the beater in the mixer with a spatula.
- Add flavouring and dried fruit.
- Immediately pour the mixture between levelling guides onto a Silpat baking mat and roll out to desired thickness.
- Cover the nougat with a second Silpat baking mat and leave to cool.
- Cut the nougat the following day using a knife.
- Cut in a sawing motion in order to prevent the mixture from sticking to the knife (do not press down on the knife).
- Wrap immediately or dip into chocolate.

WORKING METHOD 2

280 g sugar, 150 g water, 50 g corn syrup, 280 g honey, 150 g egg whites, vanilla or orange blossom water, 100 g almonds, 100 g hazelnuts, 40 g pistachio nuts, 100 g coarsely ground candied cherries
- Roast the almonds and hazelnuts until light brown.
- Boil the sugar, the water and the corn syrup to 130°C (266°F).
- At the same time bring the honey to the boil.
- Pour the boiling honey onto the sugar syrup at 130°C (266°F) and continue to boil to 137°C (279°F).
- Meanwhile, beat the egg whites until stiff.
- Pour the mixture onto the beaten egg whites in a spiral.
- Heat the edges of the mixing bowl with a heat gun to dry the mixture, until the nougat no longer sticks to the back of the hand.
- Replace the beater in the mixer with a spatula.
- Add flavouring and dried fruit. Blend well.
- Immediately pour the mixture between levelling guides onto a Silpat baking mat and roll out to desired thickness.
- Cover the nougat with a second Silpat baking mat and leave to cool.
- Cut the nougat the next day using a knife as for the previous recipe.
- Wrap immediately or dip into chocolate.

WORKING METHOD 3

1 egg white, 100 g sugar, 250 g honey, orange blossom flavouring, 500 g roasted almonds
- Beat the egg white with the sugar.
- Meanwhile boil the honey to 135°C (275°F).
- While stirring pour the honey onto the egg white and continue to boil to 116°C (241°F).
- Fold in orange blossom flavouring and almonds. Pour the nougat into a frame on a Silpat baking mat or on rice paper.
- Leave to cool.
- Cut and wrap or dip into chocolate.

---

[1] Honey consists of: invert sugar approx. 70%, saccharose approx. 10%, water approx. 20%, impurities, invertase, etc. The largest part is therefore invert sugar. Disadvantages: is hygroscopic and turns brown during boiling.

Fruit-in-liqueur chocolates

Principle *179* / Fruit *179* / Cerisette *181* / Cherry cordial *181* /

These pralines contain a liqueur-saturated fruit (whole or part), floating in sugar syrup in their chocolate shell. The best known are cerisettes, but many other fruits such as pineapple, tangerines, passion fruit, raspberries and raisins lend themselves to this application. Sweet fruits are less suitable since the predominant sugar environment in which they exist does not sufficiently bring out the fruit flavour.

Principle

The invert sugar formation is created, for the most part, during the heating process of the fondant sugar and by the invertase, if this is used. This results in the sugar splitting into corn syrup and fructose, which typically pick up moisture more easily. In this process, the liqueur-saturated fruits reach a balance during migration from water and alcohol into the fondant sugar environment in which they exist, and the fondant sugar turns into a liqueur syrup.

Fruit

Home preserving fresh fruit. Home preserving fruit in tins or jars after processing. Buying jars of ready made fruit soaked in liqueur.

HOME PRESERVING FRESH FRUIT / **Two options**

PRESERVING IN JARS, WITHOUT STEMS:
Since many more cherries without stems, rather than with stems, can be preserved in a jar, you save on liqueur. Stems are dried separately. Cerisettes with stems require a lot of extra work since the stems are reattached before dipping.
Preserving cherries with their stems in jars has the advantage that they can be more easily dipped firstly into fondant sugar and then chocolate.
Preserving fruits in alcohol has two advantages: the fruits themselves become soft and full of flavour, while the alcohol turns into a delicious liqueur.
Preserving can be achieved with rum, kirsch, brandy,

whisky or vodka. The fruits must be fresh and just ripe. Fruits that are overripe will be too soft after preserving. Wash the fruit and leave to drain before arranging in jars. A few cloves and pieces of cinnamon provide extra flavour.

Recipe 1
~ Cover the fruits with approx. 50° kirsch liqueur.
~ Seal with lid and keep in a cool, dark place.
~ Allow to stand for at least two weeks before use.

Recipe 2
1,000 g 94° to 96° alcohol , 600 g water, 200 g kirsch, 200 g 30° Baumé (54° Brix) sugar syrup
~ Blend all ingredients.

Tip: Buy fruits in season, when they are cheap. Preserved in jars with liqueur, they can be kept for years.

FRUIT IN TINS AND JARS
(PINEAPPLE OR TANGERINES)
1,000 g sugar, 500 g fruit juice (if necessary add water to 500 g), 3 800 g jars or tins of fruit
~ Bring the sugar and juice to the boil. Add the fruit and continue to boil for a few minutes. Do not let the fruit become too soft.)
~ Leave overnight.
~ Cut the fruit to the desired dimensions and arrange in jars. Cover fruit with approx. 50° kirsch or cognac or as in recipe 2, described above.
~ Seal with a lid and keep in a cool dark place.

Important: To avoid the risk of fermentation in jars or pralines, ensure that the degree of alcohol is no less than 40°. If the fruits are used for other purposes than for making cerisettes (as a dessert, for example), add extra sugar. This enhances the natural flavour and counteracts the effect of alcohol, which shrinks the fruits and makes them hard. Per 500 g of fruit (including sweet fruit) 500 g liqueur and 125 g sugar is added.

READY MADE FRUIT /

Cherries in liqueur, with or without stems, are available on the market.

Cerisette

WITH STEM / **Drain the cherries in a colander.** Meanwhile, slowly heat the fondant sugar stirring well, to a temperature of 55°C (131°F), maximum 65°C (149°F). Preferably au bain marie. Reduce the fondant sugar by adding preserving syrup, until it is sufficiently liquid to be able to dip the cherries into it. A little cherry compound may be added. To improve and speed up the inverting process add 2 to 5 g invertase per 1,000 g fondant sugar. Usually the bain marie bowl is left over a pan of simmering water to prevent the fondant from cooling down too quickly during dipping. The cherries are dipped individually into the warm fondant sugar and placed on a Silpat baking mat. To prevent crust formation on the surface of the fondant sugar, stir regularly. As soon as they are cooled, the cherries are provided with a chocolate base to prevent leakage. This is done by piping chocolate drops onto a Silpat baking mat using a pastry bag, and sticking the cherries on the liquid chocolate. Once the chocolate bases are hardened, the cherries are dipped into the chocolate up to the stem and then arranged on a Silpat baking mat. Sometimes the cherries are placed on chocolate sprinkles or chocolate flakes: in the event of a leak the small sugar drop between the decoration can dry out.

Most important: never let the fondant get too hot in specific places, since the fine sugar crystals in those places will melt and new, coarser crystals, will be created. These coarse crystals will subsequently invert with great difficulty or not at all, resulting in part of the fondant sugar not turning into syrup. If the fondant sugar was too hot, a small quantity of fresh fondant may be added as a seeding agent.

WITHOUT STEM / **As above, but the cherries are dipped into the fondant sugar using a round dipping fork and placed on a Silpat baking mat.** As soon as the fondant sugar starts to solidify a stem is stuck to it. After cooling, it is advisable to reinforce the stems by piping some chocolate around their bases.

MOULDED CERISETTES, PINEAPPLE OR OTHER FRUITS / **A variation on the previous pralines but whereby the fondant sugar is only lukewarm.**
Fill the moulds and leave chocolate to harden.
Pipe a drop of chocolate onto each shell and immediately stick the cherry onto it.
Gently heat the fondant sugar while stirring up to a maximum of 28°C (82°F).
Add the preserving liqueur syrup; this gives the fondant sugar an easily pipable substance. As described above, a small amount of cherry compound and invertase may be added.
To decrease sweetness, a little whole milk powder may be combined with the fondant sugar. Approximately 50 g milk powder per 1,500 g fondant sugar. Fill the shells using a pastry bag to 2 mm from the upper edge.
Allow to crust.
Finish with smooth liquid chocolate.

Cherry cordial

Since alcohol is banned in many countries, cerisettes without alcohol are made on a different basis. Most recipes consist of fondant sugar with a high sugar concentration, and invertase to turn the cream into a semi-liquid syrup. Inversion of the sugars from the fondant, and the low dilution of the syrup in the fruit must be stabilised within a short period of time. The composition consists of candied fruit (without pips), fondant sugar, sugar syrup (to dilute the fondant sugar) and invertase. Shelf life depends on a number of factors:
- the sugar syrup should measure at least 75° Brix, otherwise fermentation or mould may ensue;
- the chocolate coating must be thick enough to prevent the syrup from drying out.

FONDANT SUGAR (WITH INVERT SUGAR)
1,000 g sugar, 300 g water, 250 g corn syrup (42 DE),
125 g invert sugar
- For working method see the section on 'Fondant sugar'.

THINNING SYRUP
1,000 g sugar, 1,000 g corn syrup (55 DE), 200 g invert sugar, 300 g water
- Bring the sugar and water to the boil.
- Add the corn syrup and invert sugar and boil to 112°C (235°F).
- Leave to cool to approximately 37°C (99°F).

FINAL CENTRE

1,000 g fondant sugar, 500 g thinning syrup, 5 g invertase

- Slowly heat the fondant sugar and add the thinning syrup. If the fondant sugar is still too thick for processing, extra thinning syrup may be added until the desired piping consistency is achieved. Bring the temperature to below 32°C (89°F).
- Add the invertase.
- Fill the moulds and allow chocolate to harden.
- Pipe a drop of chocolate onto the chocolate shells and immediately stick the cherries in place. Pipe the final centre onto this. Vibrate thoroughly to even out the cream and remove any air bubbles.
- After cooling gently heat the edges of the chocolate shells for better adherence. Seal the moulds with thin chocolate. Thorough vibration ensures a perfect seal without air bubbles.
- Preferably keep for two weeks at a temperature of approximately 20°C (68°F) before selling.

Marzipan and perzipan

13

Marzipan crunch *189* / Pistachio cubes *190* /

Even though industrial marzipan is commonly used, it is still useful to take a closer look at the production of marzipan. The quality of marzipan mainly depends on:

- The ratio of almonds and sugars 60% almonds and 40% sugars: This almond/marzipan is ideal as a centre for pralines. Other ingredients, such as flavourings or fruit purees, may be added. As this almond dough is too rich in fat, the oil is easily separated during processing. 50% almonds and 50% sugars: easier to process, and still suitable for use as a centre in pralines. 40% almonds and 60% sugars: is mainly used for decoration and figurines.
- Degree of grinding: a very fine structure is more easily kneadable for decoration and melts easily in the mouth. In a coarser structure the almonds and their flavour are more noticeable.
- Microbiological status
- Flavour, aroma and colour
- Processability

PREPARATION METHOD /

RAW PREPARATION: 1/1 RECIPE

1,000 g almonds, 200 g fondant sugar,
100 g invert sugar, 700 g icing sugar

- Place the almonds in boiling water and allow to soak for about five minutes until the shells come off easily.
- Remove the shells and dry the almonds so they are semi-dry.
- Combine the almonds, fondant sugar, invert sugar and half of the icing sugar in a food processor[1] with sharp knives. Let the food processor run for a few minutes until the desired fineness is achieved.
- Add the remaining icing sugar and run until the dough is smooth. Wrap immediately.

WITH BOILED SUGAR: 1/1 RECIPE

1,100 g almonds, 900 g sugar, 300 g water,
200 g corn syrup, 100 g invert sugar

- Coarsely grind the freshly peeled almonds in a food processor.
- Boil sugar, water and corn syrup to 120°C (248°F).
- Fold in the coarsely ground almonds.
- Pour the mixture onto a Silpat baking mat and leave to cool.
- Process in the food processor for a few minutes with the other ingredients, until the desired fineness.
- Wrap immediately.

WITH BOILED SUGAR: 1/2 RECIPE (FOR LONGER SHELF LIFE. SUITABLE FOR DECORATION AND MARZIPAN FIGURINES.)

3, 000 g almonds, 5,000 g sugar, 1,500 g water,
1,000 g corn syrup, 18 g potassium sorbate (E202) (Only if longer shelf life is required.)

- Coarsely grind almonds in a food processor.
- Boil the sugar, water and corn syrup to 120°C (248°F).
- Pour the mixture (with the potassium sorbate) into the food processor and onto the almonds.
- Process until the desired fineness is obtained.

HYGIENE / Due to its moisture content, marzipan may be microbically contaminated. Preparation and processing must take place in very hygienic conditions. Shelf life may vary from a few weeks to one year.

STORAGE / Preferably store marzipan between 10 and 15°C (50-59°F). To avoid undesirable structural change marzipan should not be frozen. Processing preferably approximately 20 to 22°C (68 to 72°F). Never process cold marzipan, as the oil is liable to separate.

PERZIPAN / Since almonds are an expensive ingredient, peach or apricot stones are sometimes used as an alternative for the production of marzipan. This is referred to as perzipan. The structure, applications and processing are the same as with marzipan. The taste is little stronger and fruitier, but also very pleasant. Because of its stronger taste, perzipan is suitable for use in bakeries for the processing of baked products such as Christmas stollen. However, as a result of increased demand for perzipan, the price of peach and apricot stones is almost as high as that of almonds. Perzipan (persicus Latin for peach) is made from peeled and debittered apricot or peach stones. Most stones come from China and Siberia. There are more than two hundred different varieties of apricots. High quality perzipan contains approximately 35% sugar and 20% moisture. In order to distinguish perzipan from marzipan 0.2% starch must be added. The production of perzipan is identical to that of marzipan.

---

[1] A robust food processor such as the Robot Coupe is required.

Marzipan crunch

Roll out marzipan to 4 mm thickness and place in a frame. Cover with
basic ganache (see p. 115), to a thickness of 5 mm. Allow to harden. Spread
a thin layer of dark chocolate on the base. After hardening cover the surface
with a thin coat of chocolate. Immediately sprinkle with *brésilienne* and
gently press in the grains. Cut immediately with a wire slicer. Dip the
crunches into extra thin dark chocolate.

Pistachio cubes

2,000 G MARZIPAN 50/50 / 350 G PISTACHIO NUTS /
200 G KIRSCH / 170 G COCOA BUTTER / 600 G DARK CHOCOLATE

Grind the pistachio nuts into a paste. Fold in the marzipan and dilute with kirsch. Next add the cocoa butter and the chocolate. Pour the mixture into a frame on a Silpat baking mat and allow to harden. Remove the pistachio mixture from the frame. Spread dark chocolate on covers. After hardening turn over once again and cut with wire slicer. Dip the pieces into dark chocolate. Garnish.

14

Truffles
and chocolate truffle balls

Praliné truffle *193* / Orange truffle *195* / Spice truffle *196* /
Lavender truffle *197* / Coconut truffle *199* / Gianduja truffle *200* / Honey truffle *201* /
Cinnamon truffle *203* / Caramel truffle *205* / Coffee truffle *206* / Mitilinis *207* /
Butter truffle with kirsch *209* / Chocolate truffle balls *210* /

Truffles

Original truffles are always piped onto baking paper in an oval or ball shape. Once the centres have hardened they are rolled in cocoa powder, with or without icing sugar. Because of their uneven and rough surface truffles were named after the real truffle, the fungus from Périgord (France). Their popularity and fast preparation method led to many variations being created.

In Germany the designation 'truffel' is defined by law. This designation refers to the centre and not the appearance. The truffle centre must consist of cream and chocolate, and may be combined with other ingredients. After the rise in popularity of the attractive round chocolate truffle balls from Switzerland and Germany, these also often carry the name 'truffel'. The advantage of these truffle balls is that liquid centres may be used. Below various truffles are discussed, regular ones as well as truffle balls.

Praliné truffles

Aw. 0,654

500 G BUTTER / 100 G FONDANT SUGAR /
500 G PRALINÉ / 800 G MILK CHOCOLATE / VANILLA FLAVOURING

Whip the butter. Add the fondant sugar and vanilla flavouring. Blend well.
Fold in the praliné and then the chocolate. Stir thoroughly and immediately pipe into long strips. Allow to harden and cut using wire slicer. Dip the
pieces into milk chocolate and finish with finely grated milk chocolate.

Orange truffles

Aw. 0,678

200 G WHIPPING CREAM / **200 G CORN SYRUP** / **200 G BUTTER** /
150 G EGG YOLKS / **200 G SUGAR** / **150 G ORANGE JUICE** /
1,700 G MILK CHOCOLATE / **200 G COINTREAU CONCENTRATE 60°**

Heat the cream together with the corn syrup and the butter. Whip the egg
yolks and sugar and quickly add to the warm milk. Continue to heat to
approximately 90°C (194°F). Add orange juice and boil for a short time.
Fold in the chocolate and then the liqueur. Leave the mixture to cool.
Quickly smooth out in a mixer. Pipe into long strips and allow to crust
slightly. Dip the pieces into dark chocolate. Immediately roll in a mixture
of dark and white chocolate flakes.

Spice truffles

Aw. 0,776

**400 G WHIPPING CREAM / 100 G CORN SYRUP /
4 G SPICE MIX FOR GINGERBREAD[1] / 900 G MILK CHOCOLATE**

Bring cream, corn syrup and spice mix to the boil. Leave the mixture until it is lukewarm before pouring over the precrystallised chocolate. Pipe into long strips and allow to crust slightly. Cut using a wire slicer. Dip the pieces into milk chocolate and place on a wire rack. Roll the truffles one by one across the wire rack, as soon as the chocolate begins to harden. This will give the truffles an uneven appearance. Arrange the truffles on baking paper.

---

[1] Spice mixtures for gingerbread mostly consist of cinnamon, orange rind, coriander, ginger, anise, cloves, cardamom and nutmeg. They are readily available on the market.

Lavender truffles

Aw. 0,775

500 G WHIPPING CREAM / **4 G DRIED LAVENDER** /
700 G WHITE CHOCOLATE / **700 G MILK CHOCOLATE** / **500 G BUTTER**

Bring the cream and lavender to the boil. Strain the cream onto the finely chopped chocolate. Whip the butter. Add the ganache to the butter cream. Leave the mixture to cool until slight solidification of the surface. Carefully blend the mixture and immediately pipe into long strips. Allow to crust slightly. Cut with wire slicer. Dip the truffles into milk chocolate. Finish by rolling them into castor sugar.

Colouring sugar
Blend castor sugar in a bowl with a small quantity of powdered colouring agent (such as Bleu scintillant DC052 by PCB). Stir thoroughly!

Coconut truffles

Aw. 0,796

500 G COCONUT MILK / **50 G CORN SYRUP** /
1,200 G WHITE CHOCOLATE / **100 G MYCRYO BUTTER** /
50 G INVERT SUGAR / **200 G GRATED COCONUT** / **50 G SORBITOL**

Bring coconut milk and corn syrup to the boil and pour onto the finely chopped chocolate. Add the invert sugar, the sorbitol and then the grated coconut. Leave the mass to cool and then add the Mycryo butter. (If not available cocoa butter must be precrystallised.)

Stir well and immediately pipe into long strips. Allow to crust slightly. Blend precrystallised 70/30 chocolate with 10% grated coconut. Immediately dip the truffles into this mixture and vibrate thoroughly to emphasise the structure of the grated coconut.

Gianduja truffles

Aw. 0,740

800 G GIANDUJA / 250 G BUTTER

Cut half of the gianduja into pieces and melt the other half. Process both parts in a mixer until smooth. If required the edges of the bowl may be slightly heated with a heat gun. (Ensure that a light, piping mass is maintained, it must not run.) Add the softened butter and whip the mixture. Immediately pipe into long strips and allow to harden. Cut using a wire slicer. Dip the pieces into dark chocolate. Use a wire rack to apply a ripple pattern before placing the truffles on baking paper.

Warning!
If the mass is overheated it will become too liquid for piping. In this case the mixing bowl should be cooled for a short time, until slight crystallisation is observed around the edges. Immediately whip the mixture again.

Honey truffle

Aw. 0,746

1,000 G WHIPPING CREAM / **1,400 G MILK CHOCOLATE** /
1,000 G WHITE CHOCOLATE / **300 G HONEY** / **100 G BUTTER** /
GROUND CUMIN / **A PINCH OF GROUND CLOVES (OPTIONAL)**

Bring the cream to the boil. Pour the mixture onto the chopped chocolate.
Fold in the honey and butter. Lastly, flavour with cumin and an optional
pinch of ground cloves. Leave the mixture to cool until solidification occurs. Stir until smooth and immediately pipe into ball shapes. Allow the
truffles to harden slightly. Dip them into chocolate and finish with cocoa
powder.

Cinnamon truffle

Aw. 0,789

200 G WHIPPING CREAM / **2 G CINNAMON POWDER** / **2 CLOVES** / **800 G MILK CHOCOLATE** / **300 G DARK CHOCOLATE** / **400 G FONDANT SUGAR** / **500 G BUTTER**

Bring the cream and spices to the boil and pour over one half of the melted chocolate. Soften the butter in a mixer and add the fondant sugar. Add the ganache while stirring and then the remaining chocolate. Pipe into ball shapes and allow to crust slightly before dipping into dark chocolate. Finish in a mixture of icing sugar and 5% cinnamon.

Caramel truffles

Aw. 0,674

**200 G WHIPPING CREAM / 20 G INSTANT COFFEE / 100 G SUGAR /
100 G HONEY / 500 G MILK CHOCOLATE**

Slightly heat the cream and instant coffee. Melt the sugar into caramel.
Slowly heat the cream and stir carefully into the caramel. Leave until lukewarm and add honey. Pour the mixture onto the chopped chocolate. Blend
until smooth and leave to cool. Whip and immediately pipe into long
strips. Allow to crust slightly before cutting with wire slicer. Dip the truffles into dark chocolate. Finish with dark chocolate flakes.

Coffee truffles

Aw. 0,697

300 G BUTTER / **250 G FONDANT SUGAR** /
400 G DARK CHOCOLATE / **20 G PURE ALCOHOL (OPTIONAL)** /
COFFEE PASTE (TO TASTE) / **A DASH OF SODIUM BICARBONATE**

Soften butter in a mixer. Add the fondant sugar in small quantities and whip the mixture. Add the chocolate and then the alcohol, coffee paste and sodium bicarbonate. Pipe into long strips and allow to crust slightly. Cut using a wire slicer. Dip the truffles into white chocolate and roll on a wire rack for a ribbed effect. Arrange the truffles on baking paper.

Mitilinis

Aw. 0,719

**200 G WHIPPING CREAM / 150 G CORN SYRUP /
1,000 G DARK CHOCOLATE / 140 G OUZO / 200 G BUTTER**

Bring the cream and corn syrup to the boil. Pour onto the chocolate and fold in the ouzo. Leave the mixture to cool completely. Fold in the softened butter and carefully stir before piping the centre. Pipe long strips or oval shapes on baking paper using a smooth decorating tip no. 7 or 8. Allow to set in refrigerator. Cut the long strips using a wire slicer. Dip the mitilinis into dark chocolate and immediately roll into flakes of milk chocolate.

Note
When using chocolate with a low PH, this centre will curdle. In this case the ganache should be left to solidify slightly on the surface and the edges of the bowl while cooling. Next mix the ganache in the machine until smooth. Pipe immediately.

Butter truffle
with kirsch

Aw. 0,642

250 G BUTTER / **80 G INVERT SUGAR** /
500 G MILK CHOCOLATE / **60 G KIRSCH JACOBERT 48°**

Stir the butter until creamy and add the invert sugar. Fold in the chocolate and then the kirsch. Pipe into ball shapes. Allow to crust overnight before dipping into dark chocolate. Finish with a mixture of castor sugar and 8% finely ground coffee.

Chocolate truffle balls

These products are originally from Switzerland, Germany and Austria. They are often referred to as truffles, although German legislation only allows the designation 'truffel' for pralines made with a truffle centre, regardless of appearance. Truffle centres must contain the following ingredients to comply with German legislation: chocolate, cream or condensed milk (providing the latter contains at least 4% milk fat) or butter. The advantage of using truffle balls is that chocolates can be made quickly without specialist knowledge. Semi-liquid centres can also be used. The expensive purchase price of the chocolate shells is a disadvantage.

The balls must be completely filled as air between the centre and cover will shorten the shelf life. (Mould will form.)

A FEW CLASSIC RECIPES /

CARAMEL   AW. 0,783

1,100 g whipping cream, 270 g corn syrup, 30 g instant coffee, 100 g invert sugar, 50 g sorbitol, 2,300 g Callebaut caramel chocolate

- Bring cream, corn syrup, instant coffee and sorbitol to the boil.
- Pour the mixture onto the finely chopped caramel chocolate.
- Blend in the invert sugar.
- Whisk until smooth and cool as soon as possible.

ORANGE   AW. 0,796

1,100 g whipping cream, 250 g corn syrup, rind from 2 oranges, 50 g sorbitol, 60 g orange compound, 50 g invert sugar, 2,300 g milk chocolate, 40 g Cointreau concentrate 60% (reduce chocolate quantity to 2,200 g if no alcohol is used)

- Bring cream, corn syrup, rind and sorbitol to the boil. Pour this mixture onto the chopped chocolate and immediately add the compound.
- Whisk the mixture until smooth and add the invert sugar and Cointreau.
- Cool as soon as possible.

CINNAMON   AW. 0,786

1,200 g whipping cream, cinnamon powder, 300 g corn syrup, 60 g sorbitol, 2,500 g white chocolate, 100 g invert sugar, 200 g butter

- Bring milk, cinnamon powder and corn syrup to the boil.
- Pour the mixture onto the finely chopped white chocolate.
- Whisk the mixture until smooth and add the invert sugar.
- As soon as the mixture is lukewarm, add the softened butter.

CHAMPAGNE   AW. 0,806

1,100 g whipping cream, 300 g corn syrup, 50 g sorbitol, 100 g invert sugar, 1,100 g milk chocolate, 1,100 g white chocolate, 60 g Marc de champagne concentrate (decrease quantity of milk chocolate to 1,000 g if no alcohol is used)

- Bring cream, corn syrup and sorbitol to the boil and pour onto the finely chopped chocolate.
- Whisk the mixture until smooth.
- Blend in the invert sugar and the concentrate.
- Cool as soon as possible.

BITTER CHOCOLATE   AW. 0,886

1,700 g whipping cream, 400 g corn syrup, 80 g sorbitol, 1,800 g 70-30 chocolate, 70 g invert sugar, 200 g butter

- Bring cream, corn syrup and sorbitol to the boil.
- Pour the mixture onto the finely chopped chocolate and whisk until smooth.
- Immediately blend in the invert sugar.
- As soon as the mixture is lukewarm, add the softened butter.

GREEN TEA   AW. 0,782

400 g whipping cream, 80 g corn syrup, 40 g green tea, 300 g dark chocolate, 400 g milk chocolate

- Bring cream, corn syrup and tea to the boil.
- Leave for a few minutes.
- Strain the lukewarm cream and the tea onto the precrystallised chocolates.
- Cool as soon as possible.

Fruit dough

Basic recipe *213* / Cassis, raspberries, strawberries or other *214* /

The shelf life of fruit can be considerably extended by boiling it in a quantity of sugar. If the sugar concentration is insufficient, an ideal breeding ground for bacteria is created. In strong concentrations sugar, similar to salt, has a drying effect, which inhibits the development of micro-organisms. The preparation of jams and jellies are a good example of this. If the natural sugar content of the fruit is complemented with the correct quantity of sugar, bacteria will not get a chance to develop.

Fruit dough can best be described as a heavily thickened jam that can be sliced or cut out. Fruit doughs can also be poured into starch and glazed. Thickening occurs as a result of boiling a great deal of moisture, glazing is mainly due to pectin[1] present in the fruits. Pectin is a gummy substance that is released in most fruits when boiling the fruit pulp. Pectin is only active, however, if both sugar and acid are present. The degree to which fruit preserves solidify, is determined by the balance between these three ingredients.

Fruits with a lot of pectin are usually sour: if they are cooked with sugar, the moisture will easily solidify. Acidic fruits include blackcurrants, lemons, gooseberries, limes, prunes, rhubarb, blackberries, etc. Some fruits contain little pectin and often insufficient acidity, this must be remedied by adding citric acid or tartaric acid or (if not available) lemon juice.

The acidity and pectin content in the fruits is very diverse. Fruits with a high pectin content include: apples, apricots, blackcurrants, lemons, cranberries, gooseberries, quinces, limes, prunes, oranges, blackberries, etc. Since apples and apricots have the least pungent taste of the fruits in this list, they are often mixed with pectin deficient fruits. As a result many fruit doughs contain a large quantity of apricots or apples, since their pectin rich content yields good results during and after boiling. If other fruits are used it is recommended to process a certain quantity of apricots in the recipe to ensure good results. Otherwise a quantity of pectin must be added depending on the kind of fruit added.

For almost all fruit preserves between 375 g and 500 g sugar should be added per 500 g fruit. Take the following factors into account during processing:
- To prevent lumps the pectin is best mixed initially with a small quantity of sugar
- Respect the cooking temperatures or degrees Brix, in order to obtain fruit doughs that are neither too firm nor too soft
- Preferably allow the fruit dough to stand overnight after cooling.

Basic recipe

1,000 g apricot pulp, 1,000 g sugar, 100 g corn syrup, fruit flavouring, matching colouring, optional: a little citric acid[2] (dissolved in a little water) or tartaric acid
- Puree the apricots in a food processor.
- Bring the fruits and the sugar to the boil.
- Add the corn syrup and continue to boil to 107°C (225°F) (75° Brix).
- Remove from heat and add colouring and flavouring.
- Immediately pour the mixture into Flexipan moulds, silicon moulds, into starch or into an oiled frame on a Silpat baking mat.
- Leave centres that are poured onto starch, to stand overnight before depowdering. Centres may be rinsed with cold water if necessary and placed on wire racks to dry, after which they may be coated with castor sugar.

---

[1] Pectin: see the section on 'Characteristics of the most frequently used ingredients'.

[2] Citric acid solution: Dissolve 50 g citric acid in 500 g boiling water. Leave to cool and store in a bottle.

Blackcurrants, raspberries, strawberries and others

RECIPE I

800 g apricot pulp, 1,000 g fruit puree,
2,000 g sugar, 400 g corn syrup, 85 g pectin,
optional: tartaric acid or citric acid solution

- ~ Combine the pectin with a small quantity of sugar (100 to 200 g) and a small quantity of pulp (500 g).
- ~ Add this to the rest of the pulp and bring to the boil together with the remaining sugar.
- ~ Add the corn syrup and continue to boil to 107°C (225°F) (75° Brix).
- ~ Despite the low cooking temperature this recipe can be cut up easily into squares after cooling. Afterwards roll in castor sugar.

RECIPE 2

(GREATER QUANTITY OF FRUITS)

800 g apricot pulp, 800 g fruit puree,
1,000 g sugar, 400 g corn syrup, 40 g pectin, 20 g tartaric
acid or 30 g citric acid solution

- ~ Proceed as for preceding recipe.

RECIPE 3

(WITHOUT APRICOT PULP)

1,000 g fruit puree (choice of strawberries, bilberries,
raspberries, guavas, lychees, plums, blackberries, peaches,
pears, green apples), 1,100 g sugar, 200 g corn syrup,
25 g pectin, 15 g tartaric acid or 20 g citric acid solution

- ~ Proceed as in preceding recipe.

Miscellaneous

Advocaat *217* / Caramel as an intermediate layer *218* /
Agar-agar jelly *221* / Frappé *222* / Marshmallows *225* /
Muesli bars *226* / Chocolate spread *228* /

Advocaat

Advocaat is an egg-based liqueur and has a shelf life of at least one year.

**10 EGG YOLKS / 700 G SWEETENED CONDENSED MILK /
1 VANILLA POD (SEEDS) / 200 G ST. REMY 60% (NAPOLEON BRANDY)**

When using condensed (unsweetened) milk apply the following recipe:

**8 EGG YOLKS / 250 TO 300 G SUGAR /
400 G CONDENSED MILK / 1 VANILLA POD (SEEDS) /
200 G COGNAC 60% OR 200 G COGNAC AND 50 G PURE ALCOHOL
(APPROXIMATELY 92°)**

Mix the yolks with the vanilla pod seeds (and sugar) in a blender. Slowly add the condensed milk, whilst running the blender at maximum speed. Add the cognac and blend the whole mixture for one minute. Pour the advocaat into wide-necked bottles and leave open for one night.

Other liqueurs such as Cointreau, Jacobert Poire William 50% and Jacobert Framboise 50% yield good results. In this case the quantities must be adjusted:
- 126 g Cointreau 40% and 74 g pure alcohol
- 155 g Poire William 50% and 45 g pure alcohol

Caramel as an intermediate layer

This caramel is used as an intermediate layer for slicing pralines or candy bars.

250 G BROWN SUGAR / **100 G WATER** / **600 G CORN SYRUP** /
280 G SWEETENED CONDENSED MILK / **75 G BUTTER** /
6 G SODIUM BICARBONATE

Bring sugar, water and corn syrup to the boil. At approximately 112°C (235°F), add the sweetened condensed milk and continue to boil. Caramel scorches easily. Avoid this by stirring continuously. At approximately 120°C (248°F) add the butter and sodium bicarbonate and continue to boil to 125°C (257°F). Pour the mixture into a frame on a Silpat baking mat and leave to cool. Fill. Leave to cool thoroughly before removing from frame.

Turn the slab over, caramel layer side up, and cover with a thin coating of chocolate. As soon as the chocolate is solidified turn over. When using a wire slicer it is very important that the hardest layer be at the bottom. Cut with wire slicer as soon as possible. Allow to reach room temperature and dip the pieces into chocolate. Caramel may soften during storage. This is why it should be cut and wrapped immediately after cooling.

Agar-agar jelly

This jelly serves as an intermediate layer for cutting pralines, for example to combine a contrasting fruity flavour with a ganache.

50 G AGAR AGAR POWDER / **900 G WATER** / **1,000 G SUGAR** /
400 G CORN SYRUP / **15 G CITRIC ACID** /
15 G WATER / **FLAVOURING**

Boil the water and agar-agar for two minutes. Add the sugar and one part corn syrup and continue to boil to 106°C (223°F). Add the remaining corn syrup and leave to cool to approximately 60°C (140°F). Dissolve the citric acid in water and add to the corn syrup mixture, together with the flavouring. Spread the jelly on a Silpat baking mat to the desired thickness.

Frappé

Frappé is a basic whipping agent that adds volume to creams and centres and makes them more fluffy. Ideal for adding to butter creams, fondant sugar dough and some specific boiled sugar recipes.

12 G HYFOAMA DS[1] / 100 G WATER / 100 G ICING SUGAR / 500 G SUGAR / 200 G WATER / 1,000 G CORN SYRUP

Mix the Hyfoama DS with the icing sugar and the water, and beat to a foamy consistency. Meanwhile boil sugar and water to 111°C (231.8°F). Add the corn syrup to this mixture. Pour this mixture onto the foam and beat the mixture into a thick foamy consistency

[1] Hyfoama DS: Natural, heat-resistant whipping agent based on milk proteins. Is used to partially or completely replace egg whites in chocolate products. Available from Quest International. www.questintl.com

Marshmallows

Marshmallows is a airily beaten syrup. During the whipping process very fine air bubbles are introduced, which considerably increases the volume. Since this foamy structure has quite a large surface, it would appear that the result is not as sweet. Spek is often used on its own as candy; in this case it is completely covered with grape sugar. There are many recipes, but they must all contain a whipping agent (gelatine, egg white, Hyfoama, etc.), a stabiliser (sugar, gum arabic, etc.), a sweetener (sugar, grape sugar, invert sugar, etc.)[1]. With dextrose sugar the mixture can be beaten longer, resulting in a finer and airier structure. Classic marshmallows usually contain: 37% sugar, 19% grape sugar, 1.8% albumin, 2.4% gum arabic, 0.5% gelatine, 39% water, 0.3% salt.

50 G GELATINE / 600 G SUGAR / 200 G DEXTROSE /
250 G WATER / 200 G CORN SYRUP / VANILLA OR FRUIT FLAVOURING

Let the gelatine soak in water. Bring sugar, grape sugar and water to the boil. Pour the mixture onto the corn syrup and blend in a mixer. Immediately add the gelatine and flavouring. Continue to whip until volume has tripled. Sprinkle grape sugar onto a Silpat baking mat. Pour the foam onto it in a frame. Smooth out evenly. Sprinkle grape sugar on the surface. Allow the mixture to stand long enough before cutting with wire slicer.

23 G GELATINE / 700 G SUGAR / 300 G DEXTROSE /
400 G WATER / 350 G EGG WHITE / VANILLA OR FRUIT FLAVOURING

Let the gelatine soak in water. Meanwhile, beat the egg whites until stiff. Boil sugar, corn syrup, dextrose and water to 114°C (237°F). Pour the sugar syrup onto the egg whites while the mixer is running. Immediately add the soaked and pressed gelatine and then the flavouring and colouring (optional). Continue to whip until volume has tripled. Sprinkle grape sugar onto a Silpat baking mat. Pour the foam onto it in a frame. Smooth out evenly. Sprinkle dextrose on the surface. Allow the mixture to stand long enough before cutting with wire slicer.

---

[1] Whipping agents, stabilisers and sweeteners: see the section on 'Characteristics of the most frequently used ingredients'.

Muesli bars

1,800 G MIX OF VARIOUS GRAINS AND DRIED FRUITS /
125 G SUGAR / 50 G MALTODEXTRIN / 150 G WATER /
350 G CORN SYRUP / 125 G HONEY / 115 G HARD /
COCONUT FAT / 4 G LECITHIN

Mix the sugar with the maltodextrin, add water and bring this mixture to the boil. Add corn syrup, honey, fat and lecithin and boil to 114 to 116°C (237 to 241°F). Pour nearly all of the mixture over the muesli. The syrup quantity depends on the kind of mix used. All grains and fruits must be covered in a thin film of syrup. Pour the mixture into a frame on a Silpat baking mat. Press down and even out using a rolling pin. Allow to set, cut and wrap or dip into chocolate.

Chocolate spread

Chocolate paste needs a shelf life of at least six months. Two kinds are available: water based and fat based. Both have positive and negative properties.

Water-based: sweet due to the high sugar quantity required for shelf life; often a stretchy structure due to the high quantity of corn syrup; some recipes tend to become grainy; some recipes are sensitive to bacterial contamination.

Fat based: less sweet than water based pastes; soft and mostly creamy texture; spreadability is influenced by temperature fluctuations; after long storage periods the oil may surface; fats are subject to oxidation, especially when exposed to light. Do not use glass jars; the texture may change over time due to recrystallisation of some fats. This is why fat based chocolate pastes must always be precrystallised before packaging.

Water based recipe
**600 G DARK CHOCOLATE / 600 G INVERT SUGAR /
200 G BUTTER / APPROX. 50 G BOILED WATER**

Mix the butter with the melted chocolate and add the invert sugar. If necessary correct by adding a few drops of boiled water (if the mixture does not have a smooth texture). 76° Brix guarantees a long shelf life. See also the section on 'Ganaches with long shelf life'.

Fat based recipes
**WITH HAZELNUT FLAVOUR / 1,000 G HAZELNUT PRALINÉ
('PRA' BY CALLEBAUT HAS A VERY FINE AND SMOOTH TEXTURE) /
250 G DARK CHOCOLATE / 250 G BUTTER**

Mix the chocolate with the praliné and add the softened butter. (17% water in the butter ensures that the paste has a smooth spreadable texture.) This chocolate paste can be kept for approximately two months in a cool and dry place.

**WITH LONG SHELF LIFE / 650 G DARK CHOCOLATE /
50 G BUTTER OIL / 50 G HARDENED COCONUT FAT / 250 G SUNFLOWER OIL**

Melt chocolate, butter oil and hardened coconut fat to approximately 45°C (113°F). Blend all ingredients. Precrystallising at approximately 22°C (72°F).

Index

Additives 26
Advocaat 217
Agar-agar jelly 221
Almond praliné 93
Almond tuilles 98
Anise and honey ganache 157
Arabe 110

Black Devils 173
Blackcurrants, raspberries, strawberries
and others 214
Boiling sugar 58
Brix - Baumé conversion
at specific temperatures 60
Butter caramels 167
Butter ganache 119
Butter praliné 105
Butter truffle with kirsch 209

Candying fruit and vegetables 70
Cappuccino 154
Caramel as an intermediate layer 218
Caramel bites 174
Caramel snobinette 160
Caramel syrups and creams 75
Caramel truffles 205
Cardamom and pistachio ganache 128
Cerisette 181
Cherry cordial 181
Chocolate caramels 171
Chocolate spread 228
Chocolate truffle balls 210
Cinnamon truffle 203
Cocoa ingredients 16
Coco Delight 150
Coconut truffles 199
Coffee Delight 124
Coffee truffles 206
Cooling 39
Cream ganache with basil 156
Crystallising 69

Different flavours in caramel creams 76
Dulce de leche 85

Egg ganache with orange 132
Egg yolk cream 109
Environmental factors 49

Factors that extend shelf life 53
Fat bloom 50
Fats 20
Feuilletine 97
Fondant sugar dough 77
Frappé 222
Fruit 179
Fudge 78

Ganache as a basic cream 120
Ganache with nutmeg praliné 144
Ganaches 114
Gianduja ganache 137
Gianduja truffles 200
Gingerbread cream 101

Hazelnut rosette 123
Honey caramels 170
Honey crunch 112
Honey praliné cream 90
Honey truffle 201
Hygiene 52

Kahlua 106

Lava 146
Lavender truffles 197
Lemon 134
Liqueur pralines 72

Marco 153
Marquise 145
Marshmallows 225
Marzipan crunch 189
Measuring equipment and conversions
for sugar syrups 59
Migration 49
Milk products 19
Mitilinis 207
Mocha ganache 138
More advanced equipment 68
Muesli bars 226

Nougat 175
Nut caramels 168
Nuts 20

Orange slices 127
Orange truffles 195
Orient 135
Other sweeteners 23
Over-crystallising and under-crystallising 37

Palet d'or 141
Piped nuts 121
Pistachio cubes 190
Pistachio gianduja 94
Port 142
Praliné cream 86
Praliné ganache 163
Praliné truffles 193
Precrystallising 33

Raspberry ganache 131
Raspberry praliné 89
Recognising cooking points 60
Relief palette 159

Saffron 149
Speculaas cream 101
Spice mixes 29
Spice truffles 196
Starting equipment 66
Sugar bloom 50
Sugar coating 81
Sugar syrups 58
Sugars 22

Tasting 29
Tea ganache 164
Tempermeter 38
Thickeners and whipping agents 26
Time – movement – temperature zone 33
Tropicana 102

Undesirable defects–what can be done? 40
Viscosity 45

Whipping agents 28

Yield value 45